DAVID EDGAR

The New Real is David Edgar's tenth new play to be produced by the Royal Shakespeare Company, and his fourth to be premiered at The Other Place. His original plays for the company are *Destiny* (winner of the John Whiting Award), *Maydays* (winner of the Plays and Players Best Play Award), *Pentecost* (winner of the Evening Standard Best Play Award), *The Prisoner's Dilemma* and *Written on the Heart*. His adaptations for the company are *The Jail Diary of Albie Sachs*, *Nicholas Nickleby* (Society of West End Theatres and Tony Best Play Awards), *Dr Jekyll and Mr Hyde* and *A Christmas Carol*. He is an honorary associate artist of the company.

His other theatre plays include *Death Story*, *Mary Barnes*, *Arthur & George* (Birmingham Rep); *Wreckers* (7:84); *Our Own People* (Pirate Jenny); *Teendreams* (with Susan Todd, Monstrous Regiment); *Entertaining Strangers* (1985, Dorchester Community Play and National Theatre); *A Time to Keep* (with Stephanie Dale, Dorchester Community Play); *That Summer* (Hampstead Theatre); *The Shape of the Table*, *Albert Speer*, *Playing with Fire* (National Theatre); *Daughters of the Revolution* and *Mothers Against* (Oregon Shakespeare Festival/Berkeley Rep); *Testing the Echo* (Out of Joint); *Black Tulips* (part of *The Great Game*, Tricycle Theatre); *If Only* (Chichester Festival Theatre), a solo show *Trying it On* (Warwick Arts Centre, Other Place, Royal Court, Traverse and tour) and *Here in America* (Orange Tree).

David Edgar has translated Brecht's *Galileo* (Birmingham Rep), *Mother Courage* (Shakespeare Festival, Stratford Ontario), and Ibsen's *The Master Builder* (Chichester Festival Theatre). Many of his stage plays have been broadcast on television and radio; his original television plays include *Vote for Them* (with Neil Grant), *Buying a Landslide* and *Citizen Locke* and his original radio plays are *Ecclesiastes*, A *Movie Starring Me*, *Talking to Mars*, *The Secret Parts*, *Brave Faces* and *Something Wrong about the Mouth*. He wrote the film *Lady Jane*.

He wrote *How Plays Work* (Nick Hern Books) and co-wrote *The Little Black Book of National Populism* (with Jon Bloomfield). He founded Britain's first MA in Playwriting Studies at the University of Birmingham in 1989. In 2023, he received an Outstanding Contribution Award from the Writers' Guild of Great Britain, of which he was President from 2007 to 2013.

Other Titles in this Series

Mike Bartlett
THE 47TH
ALBION
BULL
GAME
AN INTERVENTION
KING CHARLES III
MRS DELGADO
SCANDALTOWN
SNOWFLAKE
VASSA *after* Gorky
WILD

Jez Butterworth
THE FERRYMAN
THE HILLS OF CALIFORNIA
JERUSALEM
JEZ BUTTERWORTH PLAYS: ONE
JEZ BUTTERWORTH PLAYS: TWO
MOJO
THE NIGHT HERON
PARLOUR SONG
THE RIVER
THE WINTERLING

Caryl Churchill
BLUE HEART
CHURCHILL PLAYS: THREE
CHURCHILL PLAYS: FOUR
CHURCHILL PLAYS: FIVE
CHURCHILL: SHORTS
CLOUD NINE
DING DONG THE WICKED
A DREAM PLAY *after* Strindberg
DRUNK ENOUGH TO SAY I LOVE YOU?
ESCAPED ALONE
FAR AWAY
GLASS. KILL. BLUEBEARD'S FRIENDS. IMP.
HERE WE GO
HOTEL
ICECREAM
LIGHT SHINING IN BUCKINGHAMSHIRE
LOVE AND INFORMATION
MAD FOREST
A NUMBER
PIGS AND DOGS
SEVEN JEWISH CHILDREN
THE SKRIKER
THIS IS A CHAIR
THYESTES *after* Seneca
TRAPS
WHAT IF IF ONLY

David Edgar
ALBERT SPEER *after* Gitta Sereny
ARTHUR & GEORGE *after* Julian Barnes
A CHRISTMAS CAROL *after* Dickens
CONTINENTAL DIVIDE
DR JEKYLL AND MR HYDE
   after Stevenson
EDGAR: SHORTS
HERE IN AMERICA
IF ONLY
THE MASTER BUILDER
MAYDAYS & TRYING IT ON
PENTECOST
PLAYING WITH FIRE
THE PRISONER'S DILEMMA
THE SHAPE OF THE TABLE
TESTING THE ECHO
A TIME TO KEEP *with* Stephanie Dale
WRITTEN ON THE HEART

Lucy Kirkwood
BEAUTY AND THE BEAST
   with Katie Mitchell
BLOODY WIMMIN
THE CHILDREN
CHIMERICA
HEDDA *after* Ibsen
THE HUMAN BODY
IT FELT EMPTY WHEN THE HEART WENT AT FIRST BUT IT IS ALRIGHT NOW
LUCY KIRKWOOD PLAYS: ONE
MOSQUITOES
NSFW
RAPTURE
TINDERBOX
THE WELKIN

Jack Thorne
2ND MAY 1997
AFTER LIFE
BUNNY
BURYING YOUR BROTHER IN THE PAVEMENT
A CHRISTMAS CAROL *after* Dickens
THE END OF HISTORY…
HOPE
JACK THORNE PLAYS: ONE
JUNKYARD
LET THE RIGHT ONE IN
   after John Ajvide Lindqvist
THE MOTIVE AND THE CUE
MYDIDAE
THE SOLID LIFE OF SUGAR WATER
STACY & FANNY AND FAGGOT
WHEN WINSTON WENT TO WAR WITH THE WIRELESS
WHEN YOU CURE ME
WOYZECK *after* Büchner

David Edgar

THE NEW REAL

NICK HERN BOOKS
London
www.nickhernbooks.co.uk

A Nick Hern Book

The New Real first published in Great Britain in 2024 as a paperback original by Nick Hern Books Limited, The Glasshouse, 49a Goldhawk Road, London W12 8QP

The New Real copyright © 2024 Goodwrite Enterprises Ltd

David Edgar has asserted his moral right to be identified as the author of this work

Cover image: photographs by Hugo Glendinning; art direction by RSC Visual Communications

Designed and typeset by Nick Hern Books, London
Printed in the UK by Mimeo Ltd, Huntingdon, Cambridgeshire PE29 6XX

A CIP catalogue record for this book is available from the British Library

ISBN 978 1 83904 370 3

CAUTION All rights whatsoever in this play are strictly reserved. Requests to reproduce the text in whole or in part should be addressed to the publisher.

Amateur Performing Rights Applications for performance, including readings and excerpts, by amateurs in the English language throughout the world should be addressed to the Performing Rights Department, Nick Hern Books, The Glasshouse, 49a Goldhawk Road, London W12 8QP, *tel* +44 (0)20 8749 4953, *email* rights@nickhernbooks.co.uk, except as follows:

Australia: ORiGiN Theatrical, Level 1, 213 Clarence Street, Sydney NSW 2000, *tel* +61 (2) 8514 5201, *email* enquiries@originmusic.com.au, *web* www.origintheatrical.com.au

New Zealand: Play Bureau, 20 Rua Street, Mangapapa, Gisborne, 4010, *tel* +64 21 258 3998, *email* info@playbureau.com

United States and Canada: Alan Brodie Representation, see details below

Professional Performing Rights Applications for performance by professionals in any medium and in any language throughout the world (including by amateur stock companies in the USA and Canada) should be addressed to Alan Brodie Representation, 14 The Barbon Buildings, Red Lion Square, London, WC1R 4QH, *email* abr@alanbrodie.com

No performance of any kind may be given unless a licence has been obtained. Applications should be made before rehearsals begin. Publication of this play does not necessarily indicate its availability for amateur performance.

www.nickhernbooks.co.uk/environmental-policy

ABOUT THE ROYAL SHAKESPEARE COMPANY

The Shakespeare Memorial Theatre was founded by Charles Flower, a local brewer, and opened in Stratford-upon-Avon in 1879. Since then, the plays of Shakespeare have been performed here, alongside the work of his contemporaries and of current contemporary playwrights. In 1960, the Royal Shakespeare Company as we now know it was formed by Peter Hall and Fordham Flower. The founding principles were threefold: the Company would embrace the freedom and power of Shakespeare's work, train and develop young actors and directors and, crucially, experiment in new ways of making theatre. The RSC quickly became known for exhilarating performances of Shakespeare alongside new masterpieces such as *The Homecoming* and *Old Times* by Harold Pinter. It was a combination that thrilled audiences, and this close and exacting relationship between writers from different eras has become the fuel that powers the creativity of the RSC.

In 1974, The Other Place opened in a tin hut on Waterside under the visionary leadership and artistic directorship of Buzz Goodbody. Determined to explore Shakespeare's plays in intimate proximity to her audience and to make small-scale, radical new work, Buzz revitalised the Company's interrogation of the relationship between the contemporary and classical repertoire. This was followed by the founding of the Swan Theatre in 1986 – a space dedicated to Shakespeare's contemporaries, as well as later plays from the Restoration period, alongside living writers.

In nearly 60 years of producing new plays, we have collaborated with some of the most exciting writers of their generation. These have included: Edward Albee, Howard Barker, Alice Birch, Richard Bean, Edward Bond, Howard Brenton, Marina Carr, Lolita Chakrabarti, Caryl Churchill, Martin Crimp, Can Dündar, David Edgar, Helen Edmundson, James Fenton, Georgia Fitch, Robin French, Juliet Gilkes Romero, Fraser Grace, David Greig, Tanika Gupta, Matt Hartley, Ella Hickson, Kirsty Housley, Dennis Kelly, Hannah Khalil, Anders Lustgarten, Tarell Alvin McCraney, Martin McDonagh, Tom Morton-Smith, Rona Munro, Richard Nelson, Anthony Neilson, Harold Pinter, Phil Porter, Mike Poulton, Mark Ravenhill, Somalia Seaton, Adriano Shaplin, Tom Stoppard, debbie tucker green, Frances Ya-Chu Cowhig, Timberlake Wertenbaker, Peter Whelan and Roy Williams.

The RSC is committed to illuminating the relevance of Shakespeare's plays and the works of his contemporaries for the next generation of audiences and believes that our continued investment in new plays and living writers is a central part of that mission.

Support us and make a difference; for more information visit **www.rsc.org.uk/support**

HEADLONG

We're Headlong. We make theatre with the power to move.

Big, exhilarating productions that use the unexpected to connect everyone we reach, right across the nation. Whether a work is old or new, there are always different questions we can ask. So, our productions are an invitation: to come and see something in a new way. Join us.

Our previous productions include *untitled f*ck m*ss s**gon play*, *People, Places & Things* and *Enron*.

We are 50: help us celebrate headlong.co.uk/write-tomorrows-classics

The New Real is a recipient of the Edgerton Foundation New Play Award
The RSC Acting Companies are generously supported by The Gatsby Charitable Foundation
New Work at the RSC is generously supported by Hawthornden Foundation and The Drue and H.J. Heinz II Charitable Trust

The New Real was first performed at The Other Place in Stratford-upon-Avon on 3 October 2024, produced by the Royal Shakespeare Company in association with Headlong.

The cast was as follows:

KENNETH HELMS/JUSTIN	DAON BRONI
NATALIA BEZBORODKO	EDYTA BUDNIK
OLEG SOGOLYEV	ZIGGY HEATH
PETR LUTSEVIC	RODERICK HILL
LIUDMILLA BEZBORODKO	PATRYCJA KUJAWSKA
RACHEL MOSS	MARTINA LAIRD
CARO WHEELER	JODIE McNEE
LARRY YEATES	LLOYD OWEN
LEONID ZHUDOV	SERGO VARES

ALL OTHER PARTS PLAYED BY MEMBERS OF THE COMPANY

CREATIVE TEAM

DIRECTOR	**HOLLY RACE ROUGHAN**
SET & COSTUME DESIGNER	**ALEX LOWDE**
LIGHTING DESIGNER	**JOSHIE HARRIETTE**
COMPOSER	**MONIKA DALACH SAYERS**
SOUND DESIGNER	**MAX PERRYMENT**
MOVEMENT DIRECTOR	**MICHELA MEAZZA**
VIDEO DESIGNER	**LUKE HALLS**
DRAMATURG	**CHRIS CAMPBELL**
CASTING DIRECTOR	**MATTHEW DEWSBURY CDG**
DIALECT COACH	**AUNDREA FUDGE**
ASSOCIATE VIDEO DESIGNER	**ZAKK HEIN**
ASSISTANT DIRECTOR	**MASHA KEVINOVNA**
TRANSLATOR	**DR MIRELA IVANOVA**
PRODUCTION MANAGER	**KURT MOORES**
COSTUME SUPERVISOR	**CHRISTINA TOMEI**
PROPS SUPERVISOR	**ALISON TANQUERAY**
COMPANY MANAGER	**DAVID PERCIVAL**
STAGE MANAGER	**ANNETTE WALDIE**
DEPUTY STAGE MANAGER	**EMMA COOK**
ASSISTANT STAGE MANAGER	**ALEX JAOUEN**
PRODUCER	**JOE ROSE**

This text may differ slightly from the play as performed.

THE ROYAL SHAKESPEARE COMPANY

PATRON
His Majesty King Charles III

BOARD

Shriti Vadera
Chair

Sir Mark Thompson
Deputy Chair

Geoff Barton

Daniel Evans
Tamara Harvey
Co-Artistic Directors

Sir Nicholas Hytner

Andrew Leveson
Executive Director

Andrew Miller MBE

Amanda Parker

Winsome Pinnock

Clare Reddington

Professor Emma Smith

Mark Smith

Ian Squires

Professor Ayanna Thompson

Liz Vernon

Lucy Williams

Susan Tomasky
President RSC America (observer)

The RSC was established in 1961. It is incorporated under Royal Charter and is a registered charity, number 212481.

October 2024

*To Catherine, Michael, Adam and Isaac Dale
who gave me the book that inspired the play*

'We're an empire now, and when we act, we create our own reality. And while you're studying that reality – judiciously, as you will – we'll act again, creating other new realities, which you can study too, and that's how things will sort out. We're history's actors... and you, all of you, will be left to just study what we do.'

Karl Rove, President George W. Bush aide, quoted in the *New York Times Magazine*, 17 October 2004

'The ideals of America are now the ideals of the world.'

George H. W. Bush, Veterans Day speech, 1989

Characters

KENNETH HELMS, *35–37*
RACHEL MOSS, *39–52*
LARRY YEATES, *48–61*
LIUDMILLA BEZBORODKO, *38–46*
CARO WHEELER, *29–41*
PETR LUTSEVIC, *45–55*
OLEG SOGOLYEV, *20–36*
NATALIA BEZBORODKO, *18–34*
LEONID SERGEYEVICH ZHUDOV, *38–58*
NATTY, *Rachel's secretary, twenties*
A BIG GUY *in a suit*
SASHA, *early twenties*
TASKA, *mid-twenties*
AN ORTHODOX PRIEST
A FEMALE AMERICAN WAITER, *twenties*
CHAIR *of Electoral Commission*
A FEMALE SIGNER, *early twenties*
AN AMERICAN LATE SHOW HOST
A MALE AIRLINE LOUNGE ANNOUNCER, *late twenties*
A FEMALE AIRLINE LOUNGE STEWARD, *twenties*
JUSTIN, *forties, a reputation brand manager*
A FEMALE EUROPEAN WAITER, *twenties*
A BODYGUARD
A MALE WAITER *in Smoky Pete's, twenties*

Notes

The play is written for nine actors.

All the young people in their twenties are played by the same pair of actors.

Kenneth and Justin double. The Big Guy in a suit, the Orthodox Priest, the Chair of the Electoral Commission and other parts are played by members of the company.

The play is set in a fictional, former communist, East European country, which contains characteristics both from former Soviet countries and other countries from the former communist bloc. The year of each scene should be displayed.

In this version, the Slavic language used is Bulgarian. The English translation of the Slavic language lines are in square brackets.

A forward slash (/) in the text indicates the point at which the next speaker interrupts.

This text went to press before the end of rehearsals and so may differ slightly from the play as performed.

ACT ONE

'The assumption underpinning the international consultancy business is that the same principles apply everywhere, that a foreign country is just like another swing state, just like Ohio... For the rest of the world, the US presidential election is not just a spectacle. It is a preview.'

James Harding, *Alpha Dogs:
How Political Spin Became a Global Business*

'The illusion of choice is the most important of all illusions.'

Vladislav Surkov, Putin aide, 2019

Scene One

2002. A Midwestern university: a lecture theatre, where
DR KENNETH HELMS, *a Harvard economist, is addressing the students.*

KEN. Okay, imagine this. A time, the recent past. Across significant swathes of the world, entrenched regimes cling to power. As the gap between the benefits they promised and their actual achievements widens, young people in particular challenge those regimes. They demand individual and cultural liberation which those regimes cannot deliver.

Foreign military adventures and appeals to patriotism fail to stem the rising tide of protest. These increasingly revolutionary movements reach a climax in a year whose very date has come to define the might of its ambitions.

I am speaking of course not of one year but two.

1968: the year of student uprisings throughout the West against the war in Vietnam. 'The whole world watching.' But also 1989: the liberation of East Europe from the communist yoke. The whole world *really* watching.

And of course the irony was this. The Western student revolutionaries of 1968 were trying to overthrow capitalism. While, in the east, the revolutionaries of 1989 were planning to restore it.

So after communism fell, a group of Eastern European countries resolved to reinvent themselves as free market, liberal democracies. And to this end invited a group of smart young Americans to tell them how to do it.

Which is what we did.

Scene Two

2002. Outside the lecture theatre. NATALIA *enters with lots of stuff.* OLEG, *who has his bag and a musical instrument case, follows her on. The case has stickers from many places. Both* OLEG *and* NATALIA *are from Eastern Europe.* NATALIA *is in a hurry.*

OLEG. Miss – Miss –

NATALIA. Yes?

OLEG. Forgive that I approach you.

NATALIA. Uh – I'm kinda, in a rush?

OLEG (*the case*). I think you may leave this in the lecture hall.

NATALIA. Oh my God. Uh, thanks, so much.

She takes the case.

OLEG. Of course I read most carefully full campus guidelines on Appropriate Relational Behaviours.

NATALIA. What?

OLEG. I am not sort of guy who chases ladies out of lectures.

NATALIA. No, I didn't –

OLEG. Unless they leave behind most valuable trumpet.

NATALIA. Uh, I – You looked?

OLEG. I am so admiring.

NATALIA. It is not rocket science. You just blow. Now, look, I'm sorry…

OLEG. You know, I think maybe my country is our country.

OLEG *gestures at the stickers on the trumpet case.*

(*Slavic language.*) Da ne bi da ste ot Kosice? Az sum ot Stal'ko. [Might it be that you're from Kosice? I am from Stal'ko.]

ACT ONE, SCENE TWO 5

NATALIA (*Slavic language*). Da, ot Kosice sum. Yavno sme sunarodnitsi. [Yes I am from Kosice. It appears that we are co-nationals.]

(*English*.) But maybe I prefer to speak in the language of the country I am in.

OLEG. I am from Stal'ko.

NATALIA. What does your family do, in Stal'ko?

OLEG. My grandfather died defeating fascism. For many years my father was manager in the Red October Aeronautic Military Transport Facility Number Seventeen.

NATALIA. Which produced?

OLEG. That actually *was* rocket science.

NATALIA *laughs*.

And is now the AeroSuperCorp, own by some Americans. We are moving to Kosice when I am twelve. And you?

NATALIA. My mother runs a little bank.

OLEG. So do you like the lecture?

NATALIA. Did you like it?

OLEG. Smart Young American informs us proudly how he spent the 1990s instructing Russia, oh, and Poland and Ukraine and in fact our country, how to turn our countries into his.

NATALIA. On our invitation.

OLEG. And what d'you think about our radiant future now? In this new century? 'The end of history'? Free market heaven? In fact, to my mind, just piles of capitalist everything?

NATALIA. As opposed to piles of communist nothing.

OLEG. You like it?

NATALIA. No, I love it.

Slight pause.

Yes, of course it's brash and gaudy. Yes of course the constant showing-off. But just – the *choice.*

OLEG. Between?

NATALIA. Sushi or McDonald's. Walmart or Bloomingdale's. Sex or drugs or rock and roll.

OLEG. You have to choose?

NATALIA *smiles.*

NATALIA. What do you study?

OLEG. Politics.

NATALIA. Really.

OLEG. You?

NATALIA. Uh – Business.

OLEG. Really.

NATALIA. Yes.

OLEG. And do you stay? Or do you go back, and help to make our country work? Not just for the Americans?

NATALIA. I want to make me work.

OLEG. What does that mean?

NATALIA. It means I do not just choose from piles of everything. I can also choose any kind of person I can be.

Slight pause.

And now, I really must…

OLEG (*Slavic language*). Mozhe bi, shte se sreshtnem otnovo? [Maybe we will meet again.]

NATALIA. Yes, perhaps we will.

OLEG (*Slavic language*). Ne tuk, no mozhe bi tam? [Not here, but maybe there.] Not here but there.

NATALIA. Well…

OLEG. Maybe in Garden of War Heroes. Where I am meeting my first girlfriend.

NATALIA. I think they maybe call it something different now.

OLEG. And see if history is really over after all.

RACHEL *bursts in.*

RACHEL. So here you are, you fuck.

Scene Three

2003. A men's restroom in an American hotel. In a washbasin, a sad balloon and a party bag with the slogan: 'Todd Mead, Democrat: A Governor We Can Believe In'. LARRY YEATES, *forty-seven, is peeing.* RACHEL MOSS, *thirty-eight, has just burst in.*

LARRY. Rachel.

RACHEL. You just carry on.

LARRY. Sure will.

RACHEL. Pretend I'm not here.

LARRY. That's the plan.

RACHEL. You know we're virtually the only people left?

LARRY. Strategists. Always last to go.

RACHEL. Even the fucking candidate's fucked off.

LARRY. And why might that be?

RACHEL. You tell me.

LARRY *finishes and turns to* RACHEL.

LARRY. Because you and I could have won this thing for him. Because we were a slam dunk for a Democratic grab here and we pissed it all away.

RACHEL. By *two points*.

LARRY. Yeah, and why?

RACHEL. Why do you think? The dirty / tricks –

LARRY. Oh, so not the fact that / you –

RACHEL. Paying hecklers to go round disrupting Franklyn rallies.

Enter a middle-aged woman; in fact, LIUDMILLA BEZBORODKO.

LARRY. Franklyn, the opposing candidate.

RACHEL. That's the rallies you haven't called the venue up to cancel. And that's not to mention the imaginary 'Lesbians for Franklyn'.

LIUDMILLA *has an East European accent.*

LIUDMILLA. 'Lesbians for Franklyn'?

LARRY. And if a man can't take a fucking piss –

RACHEL (*to* LIUDMILLA). An entirely invented organisation, claiming to be an official part of our opponent's campaign, to discredit him in the eyes of his conservative Christian base. Who are naturally leery about lesbians.

LIUDMILLA. Ah. False flag operation.

RACHEL (*slightly surprised*). Yes…

LIUDMILLA (*to* RACHEL). So you are –

LARRY (*to* LIUDMILLA). The Lone Ranger. Death Before Dishonour.

RACHEL. Larry, you promised, after Illinois. No more false flags or illicit phone recordings. No more dark / ops –

LARRY. But the moment when things go seriously belly up is when – rather than saving jobs in mines and auto plants – she insists our candidate comes out for men getting married. To each other.

LIUDMILLA. Is this serious / proposal –

RACHEL. Tested, in five focus groups.

LARRY. By your girl from London, who thinks rubbers are items of stationery.

ACT ONE, SCENE THREE 9

RACHEL. She's not a girl.

LIUDMILLA. But rubbers *are* / stationery –

LARRY (*to* LIUDMILLA). Rachel's Law. Make people feel good about what they're voting for, i.e. saving jobs, not two guys kissing on a fucking cake.

RACHEL. Which went down like gangbusters with soccer moms and urban aspirationals.

LIUDMILLA. Why a cake?

LARRY (*to* LIUDMILLA). And like shit with what she charmingly describes as 'Lunchpail Losers'.

RACHEL. Oh, Larry, please. No more 'what about Joe Sixpack and the simple homely folks you hail from back in Rust Belt Michigan'. Please not your mother.

LIUDMILLA. So you are –

LARRY (*to* LIUDMILLA). And this is Rachel Moss, whose 'people' packed her off to Princeton –

RACHEL. Berkeley.

LIUDMILLA. So you are Rachel Moss?

Pause. RACHEL *and* LARRY *look at the woman again; they'd assumed she was a cleaner.*

RACHEL. Um… maybe we should just let you, get on with… / cleaning…

LIUDMILLA. I am already getting on. And you are Larry Yeates.

LARRY. And you are – ?

LIUDMILLA. I ask for you, they say you piss off to restroom with your party bag and tail between your legs.

LARRY. Yet here I am, with my tail in its usual position.

LIUDMILLA. I am Liudmilla Bezborodko. I am from former Russian colony. I write and call you both. Substantial times.

LARRY. Well, we've been kinda busy.

LIUDMILLA. Offering you work.

RACHEL. What work?

LIUDMILLA. To run the campaign for presidency of my country. Against the current president. Vladimir Novotsky.

RACHEL. My. And you're the candidate?

LIUDMILLA. No, we have candidate already.

LARRY. So you *want* to be / the candidate.

LIUDMILLA. No, my job is campaign manager. And chief spokesman, actually. Please, take this.

She hands over a card.

RACHEL. InterCapInvest?

LIUDMILLA (*taking the card back and handing another to* RACHEL). So sorry, wrong card. I own little bank.

RACHEL. Mercy.

LARRY. How little?

LIUDMILLA *makes a 'so-so' gesture.*

RACHEL (*second card*). PolTekNik.

LIUDMILLA. Political technology.

RACHEL. Moss Yeates has quite strict policies about who it works for.

LIUDMILLA. I know. You are known as most notorious liberals.

RACHEL (*nod at* LARRY). Some of us.

LIUDMILLA. I am pro-choice and for women's and gay rights.

LARRY. And your economic policy?

LIUDMILLA. Well I possess signed copy of Mrs Thatcher's memoirs.

RACHEL (*concerned*). Uh…

LARRY. How d'you get in here?

ACT ONE, SCENE THREE   11

LIUDMILLA. I volunteer for your campaign, as part of knock and drag team. We do very well.

RACHEL. And your country is...

LIUDMILLA. I say this. It is former colony of Russia. Now of course spanking-new liberal democracy. But political campaigning in our country is considerably unethical. Young hooligans are paid to heckle and disrupt opposition meetings. You book square to hold rally, suddenly square is shut up for 'vital sewage work'.

RACHEL (*with a glance at* LARRY). Sounds familiar.

LIUDMILLA. But it is by no means all. You will be up against most challenging opponent.

RACHEL. What, President Nosovky?

LIUDMILLA. Novostky. No, his Russian political technologist.

LARRY. That's a, what? Consultant?

RACHEL. I have dogs. I need a holiday.

LIUDMILLA (*hands a videotape to* LARRY). His name is Zhudov. Call by everybody the Dark Master. Please, watch this.

LIUDMILLA *hands the tape to* LARRY.

LARRY. What's this?

LIUDMILLA. Video. Illicitly recorded.

LARRY. Oh, *illicit*. Mercy.

He hands the tape to RACHEL.

I think, to play that, you need to go to Europe.

He turns to go.

LIUDMILLA. But, please, my offer?

LARRY. While I prefer to ply my trade in places where the phones work. And without what I guess is your country's highly suspect record during World War Two.

RACHEL (*to* LARRY). So how much d'ya make?

LARRY. On what?

RACHEL. Your fucking bet.

LARRY. Three thousand dollars.

Wow.

Placed when we were twenty points ahead with our base, the ordinary dime-a-dozen, dumbass Joes who worry about jobs and houses and the price of gas. Before you sunk us with gay rights. And why? Because, deep down, you think that dime-a-dozen dumbass people are just that.

RACHEL. I'm sorry. I can't deal with this. I'm getting out.

LARRY. Getting out of what?

RACHEL. This. Us. Moss and Yeates.

LARRY. You can't. You're fucking Moss.

RACHEL. Then I'll only have to junk the 'Yeates'. And 'and'.

LARRY. What, and do this on your own?

RACHEL. Why, do you think I can't?

Pause.

You didn't say what you were doing. I asked you and you lied.

LARRY. I didn't say because I didn't need to.

RACHEL. Why?

LARRY. Because you knew. Because you always know. But you can't fess up to that because that would involve admitting that the most important thing for you is feeling good about yourself.

He goes out. Pause.

LIUDMILLA. What fucking bet?

RACHEL. He always puts a bet on his opponent winning. So at least there's something to feel positive about.

LIUDMILLA. And you do the same?

ACT ONE, SCENE THREE   13

RACHEL. Sometimes. But I blow my winnings on a la-di-da dinner for the opposing strategist. If they deserve it, naturally. Now –

LIUDMILLA. What are your dogs?

RACHEL. Two German shepherds and a Cocker Spaniel.

LIUDMILLA. I have mongrel which is part Cocker Spaniel. How are they called?

RACHEL. Bobby. Frodo. Ranger.

LIUDMILLA. Death Before Dishonour.

Slight pause.

RACHEL. Yeah. Now, / I really –

LIUDMILLA. And you and Larry, you are partners too in life?

RACHEL. For about five minutes. During a surprisingly successful congressional campaign in 1992.

LIUDMILLA. Wisconsin, fifth district. And for just five minutes why?

RACHEL. Uh, we didn't, really… Listen, maybe…

LIUDMILLA. But there is now Mrs Larry Yeates?

RACHEL. Sure is. Moira. Volunteer, Connecticut, state senate, nineteen / ninety-eight.

LIUDMILLA. Ninety-eight.

RACHEL *looks at* LIUDMILLA. *Is this something she could do?*

RACHEL. So who's your candidate for president?

LIUDMILLA. His name's Petr Lutsevic. He was young dissident in communism time. Then he goes to Stanford on scholarship from Schaefer Educational Foundation and is now leading our Civic Forum party.

RACHEL. Dandy. But, even / so…

LIUDMILLA. Mrs Moss. We are young democracy. We have elections sure but they are rigged and our current president's campaign is run from Russia which occupies us during many years. Still our government is controlled by former KGB. So to put things very mildly, we need to know how you and Larry Yeates turn round Wisconsin. Even if you are now just Moss.

RACHEL. Do you know the New Coke story?

LIUDMILLA. No.

RACHEL. So in 1985, Coke is the undisputed cola market leader. It got cocky, decided to change the formula – the winning formula – remove the battery-acid tang. And it's a catastrophe. Haemorrhaging sales to Pepsi. And Larry, then an ad man, realises that it's just like politics. Coke was the incumbent, Pepsi the challenger.

Re-enter LARRY, *ostensibly to collect his party bag.*

And what does the incumbent *have* to do if they foul up? Apologise. But everybody in business says, the one thing that you never do's apologise. And Larry says: Well, you do now.

LIUDMILLA. And lesson?

RACHEL. That in politics, in Wisconsin or for all I know in Warsaw, there's always a hairpin moment – hairpin bend – where, if you spot it, everything will change. It wasn't, it is now. It was, not any more. And you want to spot that moment? You hire Larry Yeates.

LIUDMILLA. So why do I not hire him?

LARRY. Good question. Seeing as how she never won a race / without me.

RACHEL. Because in this case, 'that moment' is the *Chronicle-Inquirer* helpfully exposing Lesbians for Franklyn and our numbers drop like a turd in a well.

LARRY. And if we'd *won* by two points, would you still / be –

RACHEL. And we won Wisconsin like we always win, by making people feel that voting for us makes them better people.

LARRY. Ah, the moral high ground. 'My ethics are my only creed.' Any minute she'll be telling you about her fucking mother on the Selma march.

RACHEL. The Freedom Rides. Fuck you.

Pause.

LARRY. So that's that? Really? Leaving me again?

RACHEL *says nothing.*

(*To* LIUDMILLA.) I taught her everything she knows.

He takes the bag and goes out.

RACHEL (*answering* LIUDMILLA*'s question*). 'Lesbians for Franklyn'.

LIUDMILLA. So here's my offer. To run highly ethical campaign for candidate you really can believe in, actually. In place that needs you. Now.

Pause.

RACHEL. I'll need to meet the candidate.

LIUDMILLA. He'll love you.

LIUDMILLA *goes.* CARO *enters. She's twenty-nine.* RACHEL *tosses her the video.*

CARO. It's a VHS.

RACHEL. So do you have a player?

CARO. Maybe. Somewhere. Why?

Scene Four

2004. LEONID SERGEYEVICH ZHUDOV, *thirty-seven.*

In a few moments, we pick up that RACHEL *and* CARO *are watching the video of what* ZHUDOV *is saying. He is speaking in English.*

ZHUDOV. Ah. America. Its political technology. Debates. Spin doctors. Mailshots, photo-ops. Lawn signs. Balloons.

This country which – for the forty years of the Cold War – takes on the might of the one-party, communist state, the command economy and socialist realism, and wipes it out, with – what? Big Macs. Splashy paintings. And electing everyone from president to dog catcher. How can we not be in awe of them.

CARO. Splashy paintings?

As if RACHEL *has paused the video.*

RACHEL. Abstract Expressionism was a key weapon in Cold War propaganda. As were hamburgers, of course.

CARO. Who knew?

The video unpaused.

ZHUDOV. And of course we must follow your instructions, on this matter as all matters. But Dear West you must imagine how it is for us. We are but young democracies. We are unaccustomed to two-party systems, having many hundred parties, with yet more popping up each day.

So imagine there's a country quite nearby to Russia, which holds its presidential election soon, in which the leading parties are One Nation for its President Vladimir Novotsky and Civic Forum, the main opposition. But there are also Greens who are not green and Social-Democrats who are neither: Polluters against Climate Change and Oligarchs Against Corruption. Saying this on Monday, that on Thursday, and something opposite at the weekend.

Because, Dear West, free markets and democracy are not your only gifts to us. We have studied your postmodern thinkers, we have read your Derrida. We understand that everything is discourse, that our world is just competing fictions, a simulacrum of a copy, a tribute to a tribute band.

Not something fake and something real. All fake. All real. A hologram in conversation with a puppet. A watercolour of a shadow play.

CARO. Gimme that again.

As if CARO *pauses and then winds back.*

ZHUDOV. – something real. All fake. All real. A hologram in conversation with a puppet. A watercolour of a shadow play.

CARO. That's what I thought he said.

ZHUDOV. Imagine.

It's as if the screen goes blurry.

CARO. And this is supposed to tempt me?

Scene Five

ZHUDOV *has gone and we are with* RACHEL *in* CARO*'s office. The company she works for is called Points of View.* RACHEL *removes the video from the machine.*

RACHEL. His name is Leonid Zhudov. Russian, illicitly recorded at a seminar in Bratislava. He'll be working for President Novotsky.

CARO. Illicit.

RACHEL *acknowledges.*

So here's the thing. I'm doing a report on the prospects for Scottish independence.

RACHEL. He's on loan from Putin. Formerly an analyst with the first division of the KGB.

CARO. Then I'm taking Mum on a trip-of-a-lifetime round-Britain cruise.

RACHEL. That's your racist mum, from York-shire.

CARO. Mildly racist. And my brother's going deaf. We're learning Sign.

RACHEL. Expanding your skill set. Dandy.

CARO. Not to mention my kickboxing, classes every Tuesday. And there's another thing.

RACHEL. What's that?

CARO. I really didn't like Illinois.

RACHEL. No one likes Illinois in winter.

CARO. Speaking of 'illicit'. Dirty tricks.

RACHEL. Caro, I'm not with Larry any more.

CARO. I heard. But even so.

A bell rings.

RACHEL. Oh, darn. They're early.

CARO. Who?

RACHEL. The candidate and his manager.

CARO. *What?*

RACHEL. For information, they call strategists 'political technologists'. And pollsters 'sociologists'.

CARO. Rachel, to do this properly, I'd need six weeks. I'd need to learn the language.

RACHEL. That's on top of French, Italian, Sign –

CARO. I'm on a special vegan diet, I'm busy and this is not for me.

The bell goes again. CARO *goes to answer it but* RACHEL *bars her way.*

ACT ONE, SCENE FIVE   19

RACHEL. Well fine. But the point is, Caroline, that you and I are smart dudes and fun guys but most of all we both know how to do elections. And we're being asked to go to someplace where they don't, to show them how to run a highly ethical campaign with a candidate we can believe in, and even win. Girl, don't you feel the burn in *that*?

Now a knock as the arrivals have reached an inner door. CARO *opens it.*

CARO. Welcome to London. Please come in.

Enter LIUDMILLA *and* PETR LUTSEVIC, *who is forty-five.*

LIUDMILLA. So pleased to meet you. Ah, Rachel.

RACHEL. Liudmilla.

LIUDMILLA (*seeing the video*). You watch the video.

RACHEL. We watch the video. And this of course is Mr Lutsevic, the candidate?

PETR. Petr.

RACHEL. And this is Caro Wheeler, who's completely crucial to our campaign.

CARO. And yet not actually / available –

RACHEL. So shall we sit down? And, coffee?

LIUDMILLA. We don't need coffee.

PETR (*to* CARO). So what exactly crucial do you do?

RACHEL. Caro is a pollster – sociologist.

She gestures again for people to sit.

Please.

RACHEL *and* CARO *sit.* LIUDMILLA *is about to sit, but* PETR *isn't, so she stays standing.* RACHEL *gives a slight shrug at this situation and gestures to* CARO.

CARO. I run focus groups. What we call qualitative research.

RACHEL. Very good for salience.

LIUDMILLA. Salience?

RACHEL (*to* LIUDMILLA). Whether something the voter believes will actually affect the way they vote.

(*To* CARO.) What's those sucky issues?

CARO. Vortex issues. Crime, immigration, welfare. Sucking everything else in. I don't know quite why / I'm explaining –

RACHEL. It's also great for testing language. Spots, slogans, speeches.

PETR. Even in country whose language you don't speak.

RACHEL. Yet exactly the same principles apply. 'Just like Ohio.'

PETR. Everywhere is imitation of America.

RACHEL. That's if you actually want to win this thing.

Slight pause.

PETR. Of course I want to win this thing. The question in my mind is if I need to employ Miss Wheeler to do so.

RACHEL. Well…

LIUDMILLA. It will be helpful maybe to hear your presentation.

RACHEL. I'm sorry. We started off the wrong way round. The procedure is simple and applicable worldwide.

PETR. Worldwide.

RACHEL. Yes. You start with voter information. In America, that's census data, who people are, where they live, their gender and their age. Marital status. Voter registration gives you their declared affiliation. Then you harvest other things about them, magazine subscription lists, gun registration files. Are they churchgoers, what's their cable plan?

PETR. And?

RACHEL. And you put all those data points together, and you've got a picture of the different segments of the population and you identify the undecided voters living in the places which actually decide the outcome of the fight you're fighting. Segments like the averagely well-off suburban females we call soccer moms and she calls – Worc-es-ter women?

CARO. Worcester.

RACHEL. Or Chattering Classes or Impoverished Elders and Ms Wheeler gets a gang of them together and sits them down with coffee and cookies and finds out what – why – how they think. And what might persuade them to change their minds.

CARO. Well, really, I just listen. Give people a voice.

RACHEL. Yes but not just.

PETR. But if she does not persuade but only listens, why is it so important that we have Miss Wheeler?

RACHEL. Because, since I first saw her doing this through a two-way mirror in a British general election, I've known that she's the best.

PETR. Despite she does not come from America.

RACHEL. Because she does not come from America.

CARO. And by the way she still can't do this.

PETR. And so by the way we will consider your presentation and let you know.

RACHEL. You'll 'let us know'?

PETR. Of course.

LIUDMILLA (*reluctantly standing*). Um…

RACHEL. Okay. But one more question.

PETR *turns back, open his hands.*

It's a particular question which you must know how to answer, which a surprising number of candidates don't. Even in America.

PETR. Then ask it.

RACHEL. It's why you want to be the president. What change you'd make, what wrong you'd right. And I'm afraid that if you couldn't answer that persuasively, I couldn't take you on.

Slight pause.

But perhaps it's something you'd need time to think about.

A moment. Then PETR *sits down.*

PETR. No I don't need to think about it. In the nineties we are told by sharp young gentlemen from Harvard that it is necessary for the economy to have shock therapy. Workers are given vouchers to buy shares in their factories, which they give away for vodka. So others buy these vouchers in their hundreds and their thousands and end up as billionaires.

LIUDMILLA. Not everybody.

RACHEL (*getting out a spiral notebook*). And what happens to the other people?

PETR. No one pays teachers so they faint from hunger in the classroom. People sell their possessions in the streets. Our life expectancy declines for the first time since the 1940s. The government gives subsidies to businessmen who give them back as political donations.

CARO. So just like home.

RACHEL. What possessions?

PETR. What do you mean?

RACHEL. What do people sell in the streets?

RACHEL *noting, as:*

PETR. Little old ladies sell their dinner services and coats.

RACHEL. What coats?

LIUDMILLA. Fur coats for the winter.

CARO. And how low is your life expectancy?

PETR. What, in years?

RACHEL. Compared to other places.

LIUDMILLA. Lower than.

PETR. Bangladesh. And we are told we must increase retiring age and reduce welfare payments and charge for things that once were free. And the main cause of death of men of middle age is suicide.

RACHEL. You're in a presidential debate. You've just said all of that. You have one minute left. And you sum up. You could even try a joke.

LIUDMILLA *looks dubious about this.*

PETR. We know Marx got communism wrong. But he is right about capitalism, sadly.

LIUDMILLA. But of course, we don't want to go back to what we / had –

PETR. No, nobody wants to go back. They all want to go forward, from the old real to the new. But all of us, not just a few.

RACHEL. And that's where you will take them.

PETR. And that's where I will take them.

PETR *stands.*

Well?

RACHEL *looks at* CARO.

RACHEL. Well? Teachers fainting? Old ladies selling off their winter coats?

CARO *is wavering. Pause.* RACHEL *stands.*

CARO. Well, I guess…

RACHEL. Ms Wheeler charges eight hundred dollars a day. She will require language lessons and the address of a reputable vegetarian restaurant within easy reach of your campaign headquarters. From which we will run and win a highly ethical campaign.

LIUDMILLA. I think / that we –

PETR. I think that we employ Ms Wheeler.

RACHEL. May I ask why?

PETR. You bring us here you claim to persuade us to hire her. But in fact we are here to persuade her to be hired. And for this performance, we are just your audience. I like that very much. And we will find – or, if necessary, found – her restaurant.

He goes out.

RACHEL. The Marx joke. Shouldn't it be 'he was wrong about communism, but right about capitalism'?

LIUDMILLA. Yes. I know.

LIUDMILLA *follows* PETR *out.*

CARO. You fuck.

RACHEL. So, kiddo, how about *them* apples?

CARO. That's Larry.

RACHEL. What d'you mean?

CARO. That's what he'd do.

RACHEL. It's what my mom would do.

CARO. Your *mom*?

RACHEL. She taught me everything I know.

CARO *leaves. Enter* NATTY, RACHEL*'s secretary, with* RACHEL*'s overcoat, suitcase and computer bag, and a pile of papers.*

NATTY. New ticket, Caro's background briefing.

NATTY *hands* RACHEL *the documents and then waves a floppy disc.*

It's all on here.

RACHEL. But even so.

RACHEL *takes the documents and puts them in the computer bag.* NATTY *shrugs and goes out.*

Airport sounds in a Slavic language. Enter a BIG GUY *in a black suit with a gun-holster bulge and curly wire connecting to his earpiece.*

Good morning.

BIG GUY (*Slavic language*). Dobro utro, as sum vashiiat lichen asistent. [Good morning, I am your personal assistant.]

RACHEL. So are you my bodyguard?

BIG GUY. I'm your PA.

Orthodox church music plays.

Scene Six

2004. A side room in an orthodox church. Icons on the wall. Music from a christening service being conducted in the church. SASHA, a young man in his twenties, sits at his laptop. There is campaign stuff on the table. RACHEL stands there with her briefcase.

SASHA. Head covering.

RACHEL. What?

SASHA. It is church.

RACHEL. Oh. Ah…

SASHA *hands her a baseball cap with the slogan 'Vremeto Izteche', Времето Изтече* [*'Time's Up'*]. *She puts it on, with panache.*

Thanks. And you are?

SASHA. Sasha, Non-Violent Strategy Coordinator. Serbia.

RACHEL. Oh. Why?

Enter KEN.

KEN. Rachel. I'm so sorry. Kenneth Helms, I'm a huge admirer.

RACHEL (*shaking his hand*). Oh?

KEN. I volunteered for your immigration amnesty campaign in California.

RACHEL. From your stroller.

KEN. I wish.

(*Handing her a card.*) F4D. Foundation 4 Democracy.

RACHEL (*reading the card*). 'Supported by the Schaefer Educational Foundation.' That's Schaefer of the bank?

KEN. Sure is. And are you mastering the mysteries of Eastern European politics?

KEN *sitting with* SASHA *at the table.*

RACHEL. Kinda. But where is the campaign manager? The candidate?

Enter TASKA, *who is in her twenties, wearing a headscarf.*

TASKA. I am so sorry.

SASHA. This is Taska. She is from the group 'Vremeto Izteche'.

TASKA. You will say 'Time's Up'. You wear our hat.

RACHEL. Dandy. And you are part of the Civic Forum?

TASKA. No, we are independent youth group, in fact.

RACHEL. Uh… Youth group for what?

KEN. Taska was just released from prison, after having been convicted of a trumped-up charge of tax evasion.

RACHEL. Uh – I'm sorry.

TASKA *shrugs: it's par for the course.*

But still? Our candidate?

KEN. I understand there have been complications.

RACHEL. And 'snags' and 'setbacks'. On my first day, my interpreter was sick. Yesterday, it was her grandmother. I have yet to sit down with the campaign / manager…

KEN. They are stuck outside Dupnista. At a 'temporary roadblock'.

RACHEL. And this meeting is in the back room of a church, a hundred miles from the capital.

SASHA. Because it is hundred metres from border.

KEN. So that Sasha is not arrested too.

RACHEL. Well, gee.

Pause.

I guess we'd best begin.

She sits and takes out papers.

Now –

She's interrupted by a bearded Orthodox PRIEST, *who enters.* KEN *signals not to speak while he's in the room. The* PRIEST *finds a few towels and goes out.*

Okay. In order to identify our base and the undecideds, Caro Wheeler our sociologist has been breaking up your population into groups. So, for instance, the president's base includes small family businesses and what we call rust-belt nostalgics, we've got humanist intelligensia and creative enterprise and our targets are the struggling middle and precarious professionals. And Caro has been testing advertising spots and slogans with focus groups drawn from these segments, with the aim not just of defeating Novotsky but also neutralising the – many – other opposition parties. Some of which are kinda weird.

The others look at each other. Most of those parties are kind of weird.

So, we are losing votes to the Greens, who are running spots about saving butterflies and dolphins, which is kinda odd as their candidate's a businessman whose company is pumping CO_2s into the atmosphere like it's going out of fashion.

TASKA. Naturally.

RACHEL. But they're at eight per cent. And there's Motherland, whose candidate is last year's Miss Universe and appears to have no ground campaign at all. Yes?

KEN. Of course.

RACHEL. But the weirdest one of all is Civic Faction – we of course are 'Civic Forum' – which is run by someone called Petro Lutsenvic, who we think is taking most of his five points from folk who think he's Petr.

TASKA. Exactly so.

RACHEL. Exactly?

TASKA. That's why the party is invented.

RACHEL. Invented?

SASHA. They are all fakes. Created by the President's adviser, Leonid Zhudov. To split the opposition vote.

Pause.

RACHEL. Right.

Pause.

And are you saying that the other weird / parties –

TASKA. Well, the party with the leader's name that sounds like Lutsevic is created for that purpose also. We call clone party.

RACHEL. And Motherland?

TASKA. Is called sofa party.

RACHEL. What?

SASHA. You can fit all members on one sofa.

RACHEL (*on her back foot*). And Socialist Renewal?

TASKA. Former communists.

RACHEL. Yes, I know / that –

KEN. That's real.

TASKA. Though if not existing Zhudov would create. To remind the population of the danger of returning back to communism. We call 'scarecrow party'.

Pause.

RACHEL. I see.

Slight pause. The others are surprised RACHEL *didn't know this.*

I hadn't quite… got this.

TASKA. Perhaps you fail to take Leonid Zhudov seriously.

RACHEL. No. I think I failed to take him literally.

SASHA. And the other –

He's interrupted by the PRIEST *coming in for another pile of towels. As he goes out, he explains:*

PRIEST (*Slavic language*). Krushtenie. [Christening.]

SASHA (*to* RACHEL). Christening.

The PRIEST *goes out.*

And the other thing we must take seriously is what happens after.

RACHEL. After what?

SASHA. After the election.

RACHEL. What, in the count?

TASKA. The streets.

Slight pause.

RACHEL. Listen. I'm just a political strategist. I don't do 'after'. I leave that to whoever's won.

SASHA. Yes, well, things are maybe a bit kinda different here.

RACHEL. Clearly.

TASKA. Whoever wins does not every time become the government.

She looks to SASHA.

SASHA. Like in Serbia when the president rigs results of his election so when we get results of real exit poll – which F4D finances – many thanks – which shows the real result, we occupy the main square of the capital and we overthrow him. What we call 'Bulldozer Revolution'.

TASKA. And we must now prepare if necessary here.

RACHEL. What?

LIUDMILLA *and* CARO *are hurriedly admitted by the* PRIEST, *who looks to* TASKA, *who throws him another towel.*

LIUDMILLA. We are so sorry.

RACHEL. Caro.

PRIEST (*Slavic language*). Bliznatsi. [Twins.]

He goes out, as:

TASKA. Twins.

LIUDMILLA. I'm so sorry. There are roadblocks.

KEN *stands.*

KEN. Did they say why?

CARO. There's a 'clamp-down on cigarette smuggling in the border area'.

Everyone knows what that means.

RACHEL. And Petr?

LIUDMILLA *and* CARO *sit at the table.*

LIUDMILLA. He addresses open-air meeting in Novi Brod town square, which surprise surprise is occupied by travelling circus.

RACHEL. Caro, we seem to be involved in the preparation of an insurrection.

Pause.

SASHA. Not an insurr/rection –

RACHEL. And personally, as I've just explained, I don't do insurrections.

She stands.

After, before or particularly during.

KEN *sits.*

KEN. Nonetheless, I understand that Caro's done some work on that for you.

RACHEL. Oh, has she now.

CARO *takes notes out of her case.*

CARO. I tested out some wording.

KEN. Just in case.

RACHEL sits.

RACHEL. What, for spots?

CARO. No, for walls.

RACHEL. Like, billboards?

CARO. More like, painting.

RACHEL. You've been testing graffiti?

CARO. Yes.

KEN. 'The Whole World is Watching.'

LIUDMILLA. 'Vlad the Bad.'

RACHEL (*to* LIUDMILLA). And that works in your language?

TASKA (*obvious*). It isn't in our language.

SASHA. CNN.

CARO. And we did this other thing, which was a gesture.

RACHEL. You've been testing gestures.

CARO. Gestures which people can use in public places.

RACHEL: *'The finger?'*

RACHEL. Like this?

CARO. More –

Thumbs up.

– or –

Hippy V.

But –

Thumbs up.

– is hard to paint, and –

Hippy V.

– was used by the Soviets in World War Two. So we tried a kind of tick.

RACHEL. You're testing ticks.

SASHA. Like Nike.

CARO. No, more angular.

Thumb and forefinger. People try it and like it.

TASKA. And you test title?

RACHEL. What for?

LIUDMILLA. For the strategic non-violent resistance.

KEN. Should it prove necessary.

RACHEL. 'Resistance.' And?

CARO. Well, we tried out colours.

TASKA. And some words are dandy because they give you a colour and a flower, like Rose.

RACHEL. Georgia.

SASHA. Or a fruit like Orange in Ukraine.

CARO. Because a colour you can use for everything.

RACHEL. You could paint the tick in it.

CARO. For sure.

RACHEL. And still I wonder what this has to do with a political campaign.

KEN. F4D is one of many international organisations which are supporting these and other people fighting for the right to do what we do every four years without thinking. I think we hoped – assumed – you'd be up for that.

RACHEL. Of course I'm up for that.

She breathes deeply before continuing.

So, title.

LIUDMILLA. But may be we might also / talk about –

But the PRIEST *enters and selects* TASKA *to whisper to.*

RACHEL. And doubtless everyone agreed that, should there be non-violent whatever, that would demonstrate a real need for change. A new start. A new morning. Sunny. Spring. And the election is in May. What did they go for? Lemon? Saffron? Sunshine?

CARO. Sunflower.

RACHEL (*pleased she got so close*). Right. Cute. But / still –

LIUDMILLA. Caro –

TASKA (*to* RACHEL). Rachel. Your tyres are slashed.

RACHEL. What?

TASKA. Driver was at lunch.

KEN. Holy shit.

RACHEL. Who did this?

TASKA. I would say the people who set up the roadblock, presumably.

SASHA (*stands, in Russian*). Ya dolzhen idti. [I need to go.]

RACHEL. But what –

SASHA *collects up his stuff,* TASKA *following.*

TASKA (*to* SASHA, *in Russian*). Ya otvezu tebya drugoy dorogoy do granitsy. [I'll take you a different way to the border.]

(*To the rest.*) I take Sasha to the border. There is a garage round the corner which can fix the tyres.

PRIEST (*Slavic language*). No triabva da trugvate vednaga. [But it's necessary for you to go now.]

TASKA. But he needs for you to go.

SASHA. So good to be meeting you. I'm sorry.

SASHA *goes out, followed by the* PRIEST. TASKA *gives the tick sign and follows, bumping into* PETR *entering. She goes on out.*

RACHEL. Petr. You made it.

PETR. I hit a problem.

RACHEL. Join the club.

Everyone is standing.

How was the rally?

PETR. Police surrounding. Most people leave. What is happening here?

LIUDMILLA is speaking quietly to KEN.

RACHEL. Well, tyres are being slashed. And we have to leave.

PETR (*getting out his phone and making a call*). Then I tell my driver.

LIUDMILLA (*distinctly*). But maybe – Look. There is something else we must discuss.

PETR on the phone. CARO looks concerned, if not embarrassed.

PETR (*Slavic language, on phone*). Triabva vednaga da se vurnem v Kosice. Da, mislim che e politsiiata. [It's necessary for us to return to Kosice now. Yes, we think it's the police.]

RACHEL. What's that?

LIUDMILLA. Caro's other testing.

RACHEL. Other testing?

CARO. What, now?

LIUDMILLA won't answer while PETR is phoning.

PETR (*Slavic language*). Oglezhdaite se, idvam sled malko. [Keep your eye out, I'll come to you in a minute.]

He finishes his call, makes to go, picks up the atmosphere.

What's happening?

RACHEL. Caro? What 'other testing'?

The sound of a police siren. The PRIEST re-enters.

PRIEST (*Slavic language*). Molia vi, trugvaite vednaga.
[Please, go. Right away.]

CARO. We can't discuss this now.

PETR. Why not?

LIUDMILLA (*Slavic language*). Samo dve minuti, molia vi!
[We will be two minutes. Please.]

The PRIEST *reluctantly leaves.*

PETR. What's this? Caroline?

CARO (*reluctantly*). Ken asked me to reconvene my groups.

PETR. Ken?

RACHEL. Oh, did he now.

PETR. Yes?

CARO. We did the usual things – what animal does he remind you of, what car –

RACHEL. Speaking of cars…

PETR. What animal?

CARO *looks at* LIUDMILLA *in some despair.*
LIUDMILLA *spreads her hands: 'Go ahead.'*

CARO. Your animal was a giraffe.

RACHEL. 'Far-seeing'?

CARO. 'Haughty.' 'Superior.' And the people who say that, say 'like lots of former dissidents'. 'Holier-than-thou.'

PETR. Well then we discuss how we / turn this round.

RACHEL. Should we not go?

CARO. And then – I tested someone else.

PETR. Someone else?

CARO. Someone who's not running.

RACHEL. You did what?

CARO. But is in the public eye.

PETR. And who is it?

The PRIEST *re-enters.*

PRIEST (*Slavic language*). Kazakha mi, che politsiiata idva. Nastoiavam vednaga da napusnete. [They tell me that the police are coming. I insist you leave at once.]

CARO. The police.

RACHEL. Then we must continue this elsewhere.

KEN. Sure. Right.

Everyone except PETR *making to go.*

PETR. Who was the someone else?

Scene Seven

A petrol station cafeteria, on the road to the capital. Cars whizzing past. CARO, KEN, RACHEL, LIUDMILLA *and* PETR.

LIUDMILLA. It's me.

PETR. It's *you*?

CARO. Chief spokesman. Always on the television.

LIUDMILLA. And Novotsky beats you by four points. And I beat him by three.

She nods to CARO, *who hands data printout to* PETR.

RACHEL. This is a *coup d'état*.

LIUDMILLA. It is Caro, doing her job.

RACHEL. So, we dump our candidate for a woman who has Mrs Thatcher's memoirs on her bedside table.

LIUDMILLA. Not on my / bedside –

PETR. Who told you to do this?

CARO. Ken. But I would have done it anyway.

PETR. And I am not the candidate for Civic Forum?

LIUDMILLA. She is saying – maybe – not any more.

PETR. And who decides this?

KEN's phone goes.

KEN (*phone*). Ken Helms?

RACHEL. Look. This meeting should have happened – in Kosice – on day one. The hotel's – fine, thanks – but the phones are intermittent and the fax machines aren't even that. I have yet to meet my perennially absent interpreter. Now you are proposing changing candidate.

KEN (*phone*). Today?

PETR (*the data*). Yes, of course. And I know how people talk of 'haughty dissidents'. But in 1989, I speak at the first-ever open, public meeting of the democratic opposition, the first to say 'Soviets, go home', before our great statue of the Angel of the Nation. I am young, I'm from little village, I am nervous. I am standing with brave men and women who have spend much of their adult lives in camps.

KEN (*phone*). And where do you hear this?

PETR. And after I make my speech one of these great people comes to me, straightens my tie, and corrects my pronouncing of a phrase.

KEN (*phone, ending the call*). I'll call you back.

PETR. And yes, as you say, people / call –

KEN. I'm sorry, there's some news about a journalist.

RACHEL. A journalist.

KEN. He was planning running something about Novotsky / Zhudov's dirty ops.

RACHEL. Good, but the point –

KEN. He was found dead this morning in his apartment. Gunshot wounds, to the head. The police are saying it was suicide.

CARO. Gunshot wounds? Wounds, plural?

KEN. Yuh.

LIUDMILLA. Four points behind.

Everyone looks at PETR. *After a pause:*

PETR. We squabble, and Novotsky cheers.

Pause. He might touch his tie.

And yes there are haughty dissidents. But not me. Therefore I give my solemn word. I will consult. If my team, my people think that you should run, I will not run against you. For would that be ethical? We meet in Kosice.

(*Slavic language.*) Dovizhdane. [Goodbye.]

He hands the data to RACHEL *and goes out.*

KEN. It'll take him three days.

RACHEL. And talking of ethical. We rightly complain about Novotsky's dirty ops. How dirty is what's just happened here?

LIUDMILLA. What is happening? I tell you. Trying to do best for our people. And yes to jump-start economy since so many years of corruption and stagnation is quite difficult, but necessary to my mind. As Mrs Thatcher finds. And what stand in front of that is President Novotsky. And his secret police who are hand in hand with Russian mafia. And anyone not interested in getting rid of that, yes, maybe, they are better going home.

RACHEL. So, what, I'm fired?

LIUDMILLA *gives an affirmative shrug and makes to go.*

CARO. Uh, no. She isn't. Sorry.

Slight pause.

Cos here's the thing. If you still want me – which I think you do – we're kind of, like, a team?

LIUDMILLA. Really?

RACHEL. Really?

CARO. Yes.

Pause.

RACHEL (*with the data*). At a glance I'd say Novotsky's numbers among strugglers and the rural poor are soft. We shouldn't give up on small businesses. We should emphasise your backstory, including the achievements of your not-so-little bank. But the main thing is: no tyre-slashing, no murders, and no mafia. No returning to the old real. We can't play this election as a choice between two legitimate democratic candidates. It's a referendum on a criminal autocracy. And if we make it that, he's toast.

Pause.

LIUDMILLA. Then we might ask for enthusiasm and commitment to the candidate, and to be frank not telling us every five minutes how backwards and incompetent we are.

(*To* KEN.) When we first meet, she thinks I am the cleaner.

She goes out, followed by KEN. RACHEL *looks at* CARO, *who shrugs and follows, as* LARRY *enters with a cocktail.*

LARRY. So how's it going?

Scene Eight

2004. A Democrat event during the American presidential race. Big signs: 'John Kerry: The Real Deal'. As two bar stools appear, LARRY *walks forward to* RACHEL *with his cocktail.* RACHEL *is thrown by seeing* LARRY.

RACHEL. Larry. How's tricks?

LARRY. Just dandy. All good in Whateverstan?

RACHEL. It's not a Stan.

LARRY. And how's your candidate?

RACHEL. Long story. How's working for Kerry?

LARRY. Well, he's pro-gun control, abortion and abolition of the death penalty. Great with the urban aspirationals. Less so with our base.

RACHEL. Abortion? Isn't Kerry Catholic?

LARRY. Hence the excommunication threat. How are the dogs?

RACHEL. Tonto's got arthritis. Why d'you ask?

LARRY. I wanted to ask something that you'd answer.

RACHEL. Would I like a drink?

LARRY *waves for a waiter, gets an 'in a minute' gesture and gives a thumbs up. He sits on the stool.*

LARRY (*gesturing the room*). And why – ?

RACHEL. I'm speaking to an EMILYs List break-out group.

LARRY. Of course. What about?

RACHEL. My experiences in Whateverisn'tactuallyastan.

LARRY. And its ups and downs?

A pause. RACHEL *sits.*

RACHEL. We've had a little local difficulty.

LARRY. With?

RACHEL. The candidate.

LARRY. Peter Lutsomething.

RACHEL. No longer.

LARRY. And who's it now?

RACHEL. You could google it.

LARRY (*angry*). Yes I suppose I fucking could.

Slight pause.

RACHEL (*a little apologetic*). We're just ahead. So how's every little thing with you?

LARRY. Just fine.

RACHEL. Great. Moira?

LARRY *doesn't reply.*

Believe it or not, the new candidate's the 'restroom-cleaning lady'. She creamed Lutsevic in the polls.

LARRY. And you dump your candidate the former dissident and take up with a banker. Exactly how ethical is that?

RACHEL. Oh for fuck's sake.

LARRY. And President Novotsky?

RACHEL (*surprised and a little suspicious at* LARRY's *homework*). He's got the oligarch class and traditional conservatives. While we're scooping up the humanist intelligensia. And urban business, actually. Which doesn't raise an eyebrow over there cos unlike the Democrats and the Republicans their parties are invented election by election and their platforms can be anything they damn well please.

LARRY. Well, lucky them.

RACHEL. But the familiar thing with Novotsky is his slavish following of your playbook. Particularly adept at false flag operations. Clearly he knows all about 'Lesbians for Franklyn'.

LARRY. You could try 'Nazis for Novotsky'.

A female WAITER *has arrived. She wears a big Kerry button.*

WAITER. Now can I get you good folks anything?

LARRY. I could use another Cuba Libre.

WAITER. And ma'am?

RACHEL. In fact, I think I'm on my way.

WAITER. No problem.

LARRY (*to* the WAITER). And you're good with Kerry.

WAITER (*obvious*). Sure.

LARRY. Why?

WAITER. Gun control. Choice.

LARRY. Any weak spots?

WAITER. It'd be cool if he came out for gay marriage.

LARRY. And saving jobs in the auto industry?

WAITER (*a bit shruggy*). Yeah, sure.

LARRY. And taxing gas to pay for it?

Slight pause.

WAITER. My dad runs a trucking company.

LARRY. Ah.

WAITER (*to* RACHEL). Now you're sure I can't persuade…?

RACHEL. Why not. His tab. I'll have a gin and tonic.

WAITER. Coming up.

The WAITER *goes out.*

LARRY. 'G and T.' How British.

RACHEL. Cuba Libre?

LARRY. Rum and Coke.

RACHEL. Rum and Coke.

LARRY. Free country.

Slight pause.

RACHEL. But, even so, you don't see people drinking Coke with gin.

LARRY. Your point?

RACHEL. Like, if you think of party platforms.

LARRY. Party platforms?

RACHEL. Yeah yeah, and how it's a kind of law that Democrats are pro-tax and welfare and anti-guns and pro-choice. As if you had to have gin with tonic, or rum with Coke, but you couldn't have rum with tonic.

LARRY. And rum's gay rights and tonic's lower taxes.

RACHEL. Or cutting welfare. 'Xactly.

Pause. They look at each other.

LARRY. Hey. Old Team.

RACHEL *looks away.*

RACHEL. But in fact, now, over there, no one's vexed by taxes or abortion or gay marriage, they just want to get rid of an autocratic president who's as corrupt as fuck and in the pocket of the mafia. And we're making the election a referendum on just that.

The WAITER *is there with the drinks.*

WAITER. Uh, this is here?

RACHEL. Not yet.

WAITER. Then one gin and tonic and one Cuba Libre. And some chips. Enjoy.

She goes out. As LARRY *lifts his glass,* RACHEL *glances at her watch.*

RACHEL. Shit, I'm late for Emily.

She knocks back half the gin.

Sorry.

She goes out quickly.

LARRY. But they might be vexed about abortion and gay rights tomorrow.

He knocks back the rest of RACHEL*'s gin and tonic, as* CARO *bursts in.*

CARO. Tuesday's poll.

Scene Nine

May 2004. City hotel, campaign HQ. Busy and noisy. On screens: the CHAIR *of the Electoral Commission announcing results. A* FEMALE SIGNER *interpreting. Phones ringing from adjoining spaces.* RACHEL *has entered, taking her coat off, and starts following the results on the screen and on her laptop. Other campaign* VOLUNTEERS *rush in and out, handing* CARO *papers, finding documents, thumbtacking lists on notice boards, and rushing out again. They include* SASHA *and* TASKA. CARO *has just come in.*

RACHEL. What's that?

CARO. President Novotsky's lead in the last official poll. On Tuesday.

RACHEL. Uh – two-point-five?

CARO. And just now, that's how they're calling the overall result.

RACHEL. Surprise surprise.

CARO. So where's our exit poll?

RACHEL. Not through yet.

SASHA *passes.*

SASHA. Voters photographing ballot papers. Results filled out in pencil.

SASHA *goes out.*

RACHEL. This is crazy. You don't rig elections on the day.

CARO *answers a call.*

CARO (*Slavic language*). Allo? [Yes?]

RACHEL. Novotsky's problem: Zhudov didn't give him enough votes in his fake polls to justify what he needs to claim now.

CARO (*to* RACHEL). He didn't factor in the change of candidate.

(*Phone.*) What are carousels?

RACHEL. Which is why our numbers are so good in the city.

CARO (*to* RACHEL). Humanist intelligentsia and precarious professionals. Told you so.

(*Phone.*) Great. Thanks. And you.

Ends call. TASKA *passes.*

TASKA. Carousels, all over Province Zlin.

RACHEL. Carousels?

TASKA. Groups going round in vans and vote in different places. They are paid by vote.

CARO. Hence photographing ballot papers.

TASKA. They are told to say it is souvenir.

TASKA *goes out, as* CARO's *phone goes, and she answers.*

CARO. Allo?

RACHEL (*computer*). Now he's claiming eighty-six per cent of half a million votes in the last two hours. All in the east, including Zlin and – Stal'ko? Trying to catch up.

RACHEL *looks at the TV screen.*

CARO (*Slavic language*). I kude e tova? [And this is where?]

RACHEL. Hey. Can you understand the signer?

CARO. It's not British Sign, Rachel.

(*Slavic language, phone.*) Mersi. Obadi mi se posle. [Thanks. Call me later.]

She ends the call, as SASHA *crosses.*

At the same time, the SIGNER *on the television takes out her phone and looks at a message.* RACHEL *doesn't notice this.*

SASHA. International observers kept too far back to see the ballot papers. They are forbid to check the ballot box in military barracks.

CARO *is looking at the* SIGNER.

RACHEL. Aren't they complaining?

SASHA. Sure they're complaining.

RACHEL. Of course, you can get a late surge from one side. It isn't necessarily a fraud.

SASHA (*dismissively*). 'Late surge.'

He goes out.

CARO. 'We have the exit poll.'

RACHEL. We have?

CARO (*standing*). 'The election's fraudulent. Ballot boxes have been stuffed.'

RACHEL. What does it say?

CARO. 'Tell everyone you know.'

RACHEL. Say again?

CARO. 'Go to October Square.'

RACHEL. What?

CARO. It's the signer. 'Make this the beginning of a new reality.'

RACHEL. But you said she wasn't signing in British / Sign.

CARO. She is now. 'When they work out what I'm saying – '

The screen goes blank.

' – you won't see me any more.'

CARO's phone and other phones in the room and beyond it all start ringing. CARO answers. SASHA and TASKA rush in.

CARO (*phone*). Hi.

TASKA. We've got the exit poll.

RACHEL. And the result?

SASHA. We're five points ahead.

CARO. Liudmilla five points ahead!

ACT ONE, SCENE NINE

She ends the call. The news is on RACHEL*'s laptop now.* CARO*'s phone goes again.* SASHA *and* TASKA *hurry out.*

RACHEL. Holy shit.

CARO (*phone*). Yes, I know. I'm on my way.

CARO *finds her coat.*

RACHEL. Fifty emails in the last two minutes. How d'you like *them* apples.

CARO *putting on her coat.*

Where are you going?

The CHAIR *appears on the screen again. There is no* SIGNER.

CARO. Where do you think? I'm going to the square.

RACHEL. Caro, it's the middle of the night. And we've got work to do.

CARO. You bet. You coming?

RACHEL. Absolutely not. I'm running a democratic procedure.

CARO. So am I.

Makes to go, turns back.

Hey. What your mum'd do.

She hurries out. RACHEL *alone.* KEN *appears.*

KEN. Rachel.

RACHEL. Ken.

KEN. Go Operation Sunflower.

KEN *goes out.* RACHEL *reaches for her phone.*

Perhaps there are projections of the demonstration in the square; newsreel of international support for protests; graffiti in the language of the country and in English. CARO *appears, in a yellow sweatshirt with the Sunflower tick, carrying tent poles in bits and with an instruction leaflet.*

CARO. What kept you?

Scene Ten

2004. We're in October Square, a tent city. Nearby, a stage from which comes music and speeches in the country's language. PROTESTERS *move round, distributing food and drink, as well as banners, gas canisters, sleeping bags. A lot of the* PROTESTERS *wear Sunflower scarves across their faces. Bits of a tent on the ground.*

RACHEL. This is your tent?

CARO. It's my tent now. A job lot of five hundred, just arrived from Dusseldorf.

    CARO *kneels to work.*

RACHEL. Mercy.

    RACHEL *kneels down to help. A man with a scarf across his face is nearby.*

Assemble the poles?

CARO. Right.

As they work:

RACHEL. Why are people wearing scarves across their faces?

CARO. They've just announced there may be tear gas.

A bell tolls the hour.

Oh, shit.

RACHEL. What's wrong?

CARO. I'm running a self-defence class, in the Palace of Culture.

RACHEL. Kickboxing.

CARO. Yes.

RACHEL. No doubt going down excellently well with the precarious professionals.

CARO (*standing*). You bet.

RACHEL. Look –

The amplified sound ceases, so the speech carries on, much quieter in acoustic.

What's that?

CARO. They cut the power. It's okay, though, people come round shouting out the news. They call them human amplifiers.

RACHEL. Sweet. And hi.

CARO. And congratulations.

RACHEL. Why, what for?

CARO. You won.

RACHEL. We won. Now we have to make it stick.

CARO. With the whole world watching. International campaign. Geldof and Madonna. Wonder who set that up.

RACHEL. Someone may have made some calls.

CARO smiles, and hands RACHEL the instructions.

CARO (*in German*). Anweisungen. [Instructions.]

RACHEL. And, hey, get me a sweatshirt.

CARO gives the tick sign and goes out. RACHEL back to the tent.

(*In German.*) 'Stecken Sie die Stangen in die Hulsen.'

She attempts to insert the poles into the sleeves.

Poles into holes? Hmph.

The man in the scarf comes to her. It's ZHUDOV.

ZHUDOV. 'Sleeves.' You have a problem?

RACHEL. Let's call it a challenge.

ZHUDOV. Maybe I may help you.

RACHEL. You sure can.

ZHUDOV kneels and helps.

ZHUDOV. The trick is to feed the material on to the poles in short bits, like ruffles.

As they work:

Under communism, an insurmountable problem was a 'temporary setback'. Whereas for you it's a 'challenge'.

RACHEL *laughs.*

RACHEL. Then we fit the second 'Stange' into the second 'Hulle'.

ZHUDOV. And in my country, a demonstration is a group of people marching through the streets for an hour or two, in pursuit of a defined objective.

RACHEL. When you say 'my country – '

ZHUDOV. And here we are, occupying the central square of the capital. I wonder, would that be allowed in London, Rome or Washington? I think now we bend the poles and click them into the fasteners. And some say, go further, let's blockade the airport or storm parliament. Others, let's join NATO, or restore the country to the eighteenth century. And there, it rises.

RACHEL. Um…

The tent is up. ZHUDOV *enters the tent to smooth out the flooring.*

ZHUDOV. So what is this? A protest or a pop festival? A performance or an insurrection? A hologram or a puppet show?

ZHUDOV *emerges.*

RACHEL. A puppet show?

She realises who ZHUDOV *is.*

So why the scarf?

ZHUDOV. Why do you think?

Enter NATALIA, *now twenty, currently operating as a human amplifier. Once she's got going,* ZHUDOV *paraphrases.*

ACT ONE, SCENE TEN 51

NATALIA (*Slavic language*). Novini! Suzheliavame za kratkotrainiia problem. Ne polzvaite mobilni telefoni ako niamate chisto nova sim karta. Spored slukhove, politsiiata ima namerenie nai-milo da izpolzva sulzotvoren gaz sreshtu sobstveniiat si narod. Pazete se sus shalove! Imame dostatuchno makaroni no ni triabva oshte olio i shokolad. [News! Apologies for the temporary setback. Do not use your cellphone except with a brand-new SIM card. We hear rumours the police intends most kindly to use tear gas on their own people. Protect yourselves with scarves! We have enough pasta but we do need chocolate and cooking oil.]

ZHUDOV (*paraphrasing*). 'Apologies for the temporary shortcoming. Don't use your cellphone except with a new SIM card' – sensible. 'Rumours of the use of tear gas.' Melodrama. And they have no more need of pasta but / they could use cooking fat –

NATALIA (*correcting*). Cooking oil. We're fine for fat.

She goes out. We might hear her repeating the announcement to the next group.

RACHEL. They call them human / amplifiers.

ZHUDOV. Amplifiers. And in this case, Bezborodko.

RACHEL. No it isn't.

ZHUDOV. Her daughter. I'm surprised you haven't met. But then you are excluded, so I hear from her mother's inner circle.

Pause.

RACHEL. You're Leonid Zhudov.

ZHUDOV. And you are Rachel Moss.

RACHEL. Yeah. Why are you here?

ZHUDOV. Why are you here?

RACHEL. I'm working for the winner of the presidential election.

ZHUDOV. As am I. I meant, what are you doing *here*.

RACHEL. The president kills journalists. How did you find me?

ZHUDOV. You make calls on your cellphone.

RACHEL. So they're right about the SIM card.

ZHUDOV *gives a 'maybe' gesture.*

And why the scarf?

ZHUDOV. Well, you know, perhaps I do not entirely rely on giving peace a chance. Even with the whole world watching.

RACHEL. What?

ZHUDOV. It is not so sensible perhaps if I am recognised.

RACHEL. 'The whole world watching.'

ZHUDOV. Which the students chant in Chicago at the 1968 Democrat Convention. The slogan is also chanted in the streets of Prague in 1989. Now here. An echo of an imitation. Dramaturgy.

RACHEL. Or you might say a spontaneous protest against a rigged election.

ZHUDOV. Spontaneous.

RACHEL. You bet.

ZHUDOV. A stage. Biotoilets. Kitchens. Bands. Field hospitals. Therapists. Self-defence protest classes. About as spontaneous as a metronome.

RACHEL. You mean you didn't cheat?

ZHUDOV. I mean that American intelligence attempts to overthrow the president of a sovereign foreign country.

RACHEL. What, now I'm the CIA?

ZHUDOV. No one thinks you are in the employ of your government.

RACHEL. Well, I'm very glad to hear / it.

ZHUDOV. However, we may take a different view of Harvard's Doctor Kenneth Helms. Who spends the early nineties teaching Russia how to do free market capitalism and ends up with considerable holdings in the Russian metallurgy industry. And whose 'Schaefer Educational Foundation' enjoys such generous donations from the US State Department. As they reproduce pre-planned, cookie-cutted, colour-coded revolutions all over former Soviet space, like productions of *Evita*.

RACHEL. Pre-planned, just like the fraud which led to them.

ZHUDOV. Naturally.

RACHEL. You are admitting cheating.

ZHUDOV. Certainly.

RACHEL. Preventing your opponent's meetings?

ZHUDOV. Absolutely.

RACHEL. Parties which are merely fronts for oligarchs.

ZHUDOV. Of course.

RACHEL. That's when they're not invented by the government.

ZHUDOV. Um, when you say 'invented' – ?

RACHEL. I'm told reliably that the only minor party not created or supported by the government is Socialist Renewal.

ZHUDOV. Well, there I must correct you.

RACHEL. How?

ZHUDOV. Socialist Renewal is certainly created by the government. It is completely central to our strategy.

RACHEL. I'm sorry?

ZHUDOV. While the so-called dirty tricks which so appal you are of course quite directly from your manual.

RACHEL. You're saying there's no difference?

ZHUDOV. I say: you say you have a perfect system, and you export it round a grateful globe. All we can do is imitate the things you show us how to do. But you will permit us just a little fun. We imitate but we also magnify, like the mirror in the fairground we show you what you really are, enlarged. Our elections are a sham, yours are a show. And perhaps, when you look in the mirror, you see yours are a sham as well.

RACHEL. And so, no true, no real? Nothing matters, everything a puppet show?

ZHUDOV. I didn't say it does not matter.

RACHEL. And if it / doesn't –

ZHUDOV. Do you know of the Protocols of Zion?

RACHEL. Yes, of course. They were / the –

ZHUDOV. The forgery by the Tsarist secret police which claimed to expose a global conspiracy by Jewish finance capital to demoralise and subvert the Christian nations and impose a one-world tyranny.

RACHEL. Quite definitely fake.

ZHUDOV. But nonetheless, for some, it fitted with the truth. Their truth. One of whom, unfortunately, being Adolf Hitler.

RACHEL. What are you saying?

ZHUDOV. What I say. You have your truth, like Mr Schaefer's convenient exit poll. But for some, maybe for those extra millions, their truth seems truer.

RACHEL. So are you worried?

ZHUDOV. What about?

RACHEL. That this may happen elsewhere? Say, in Russia?

A ping on his phone. He looks. A hint of alarm. He makes a call.

ZHUDOV. You will forgive me.

ZHUDOV *makes a call, as* CARO *hurries in. She carries a big Sunflower sweatshirt.* ZHUDOV *speaks underneath* CARO*'s dialogue with* RACHEL.

(*Russian.*) Chto proiskhodit?

Kogda eto bylo?

Byli li v etom zameshany amerikantsy?

Aha,, prisustvovali tol'ko predstaviteli evropeiskogo suiuza?

Bylo li chto-nibud' ot Condoleezy Rice?

Na chto on soglasilsya?

Kogda?

Eto potrasiaiushche. Ya tebe perezvonyu pozhe.

[What's happening?

When was this?

Were the Americans involved?

Oh, so it was only representatives of the EU present.

Was there anything from Condoleeza Rice?

What did he agree to?

When?

Unbelievable. I'll call you later.]

Meanwhile:

CARO. Rachel.

RACHEL. Have you abandoned / your class?

CARO. It's abandoned me. They're saying that the government's caved in. They're going to re-run the election. So how d'you like *them* apples?

The sound system comes back on. A booming voice, in the Slavic language, announces victory. The country's national anthem is played. As RACHEL *puts up her hand. Hand slap.* CARO *tosses her the sweatshirt.*

I could only get a three-XL.

RACHEL *puts the sweatshirt against herself, way too large.* CARO *makes a call.*

Hey, Larry. Did you hear the scoop?

CARO*'s call answered, as* ZHUDOV *finishes his call.*

(*Slavic language.*) Zdravei. Az sum. [Hi, it's me.]

RACHEL. What scoop?

ZHUDOV. Well, it seems you are victorious.

CARO (*phone, Slavic language*). Da, chukh. [Yeah, sure I heard.]

ZHUDOV *looks around, a little nervously.*

RACHEL (*the sweatshirt*). Hey, listen. Do you want this?

ZHUDOV. But is it not…

RACHEL. You don't want to be recognised. And it's far too big for me.

RACHEL *holds out the sweatshirt.* ZHUDOV *takes it.*

CARO (*Slavic language*). Dobre. Dovizhdane. [Yeah, bye.]

She finishes the call.

RACHEL. Look. I know what happened, in this part of Europe. I know about the Protocols of Zion.

ZHUDOV. Of course you do.

He goes quickly out.

CARO. Uh – who was that?

RACHEL. And what's with Larry?

CARO. Uh… you know his wife walked out.

RACHEL. Moira. Sure.

CARO. And he hit the bottle.

RACHEL. Ah.

CARO. And an opponent in a state primary in Colorado. Both in a big way. You can google it.

RACHEL. Holy shit. Poor guy.

CARO. The guy he hit?

RACHEL. No. But, yes.

RACHEL *sees* LIUDMILLA *coming in, with* NATALIA.

Madam Next President.

LIUDMILLA. And do you still wonder what this has to do with a political campaign?

RACHEL (*after a smile*). And what do you do now?

LIUDMILLA. I give a speech to my supporters.

RACHEL. Yes, but not here. And not just your supporters.

LIUDMILLA. So sorry?

RACHEL. Not in the middle of the protest. Before the Angel of the Nation. Behind you, people of all ages. Everybody waving national flags. No ticks. No protest and no party. Nation.

LIUDMILLA (*with a hint of sarcasm*). And what do I say?

RACHEL. I'm sure you know that. But I know how you should end.

LIUDMILLA *gestures for* RACHEL *to continue.*

There was a World Series playoff, baseball, and the winning home run was ruled a bad call. So the coach says to the team: 'You've won this once. Now go out there and win it all again.'

LIUDMILLA *smiles. That's good.*

LIUDMILLA. Go, Lone Ranger.

She high-fives RACHEL, *and she and* NATALIA *exit.* RACHEL *turns to* CARO *and does the tick,* CARO *does it back.*

Scene Eleven

2009. RACHEL *is being interviewed by an American late show* HOST. *She's picked up the smart, sassy tone. The interview is backed by clips of the occupation, closing with the* LIUDMILLA/RACHEL *high-five in front of the tent.*

HOST. So enough about Scandinavia and the UK.

RACHEL. And Obama.

HOST. And Obama. How did it feel to go halfway round the world, to a place you knew nothing about, and overthrow a rigged election?

RACHEL. And then to go on and win an unrigged one. Easier than putting up a tent.

HOST. And might you go back?

RACHEL. If it doesn't sound too grand, I go where I'm needed.

HOST. I know *that's* right.

Scene Twelve

2010. RACHEL's *secretary* NATTY *enters with a classier suitcase for* RACHEL, *who appears.*

NATTY. Give me your phone.

RACHEL. What?

NATTY. Give me your phone.

This has been a long battle. RACHEL *sighs and gives* NATTY *her elderly cellphone.*

RACHEL. I like my phone.

NATTY *switches SIM cards, rapidly.*

NATTY. I know. You liked your typewriter.

RACHEL. My ticket?

NATTY. On your phone.

LARRY enters. NATTY exits.

LARRY. Well, if it ain't the queen of the world.

RACHEL. Larry?

Scene Thirteen

LARRY *has ambushed* RACHEL *in a first-class airport lounge, in the eastern US. She is standing, on the way to pick up her hand baggage and go to the plane.*

ANNOUNCER. Ladies and gentlemen. This is your final call for Flight UA543 to Caracas. Could passengers please make your way to Gate Eighteen.

LARRY. You're going to Venezuela?

RACHEL. You're in a first-class lounge?

LARRY. I bought a first-class ticket.

RACHEL. You bought a *ticket*? Where the fuck to?

LARRY (*finding his ticket on his phone*). The cheapest foreign country.

(*Looks at ticket.*) Nicaragua.

ANNOUNCER. Ladies and gentlemen, this is your boarding call for Flight UA54 to Managua, at Gate Thirty-Five.

LARRY. And what's the job?

RACHEL. If I get it, two thousand bucks a day. What d'you want?

LARRY. I want to know about President Liudmilla once-a-restroom-cleaning-lady Bezborodko.

RACHEL. Why?

LARRY. Why do you think? Upcoming presidential election.

RACHEL. Mercy. You've been approached?

   LARRY *spreads his hands.*

   And they don't... The fist fight in Colorado?

LARRY. They like it. Shows I'm not a pussy.

RACHEL. And I guess things haven't been so great for you here at home.

LARRY. Why, is there a problem?

ANNOUNCER. Okay, for anyone on the flight to beautiful Caracas, now would be a great time to plane.

RACHEL. Well, we turned round this fraudulent election –

LARRY. Sure. I saw your interview. Like now.

RACHEL. Bezborodko: first term: disappointment. Fundamental problems not addressed. Allegations of corruption. Infrastucture for the – Yoofa Cup? The daughter's taken out a trademark on Sunflower Revolution merchandise.

LARRY. Smart move. And the crash?

RACHEL. '08 was not a great year for the currency. Not helped by leaked tapes of ministers describing how much they'd have to lie to win the upcoming election. While enjoying their champagne at Davos.

LARRY. But you're sitting this one out.

RACHEL. I hope I'm otherwise engaged.

LARRY. And is your rubber lady still on the scene?

RACHEL. Her name's still Caroline. Yes, she's still there.

LARRY. Polling. Groups.

RACHEL. Some interesting data.

LARRY. You've seen it?

RACHEL. She values my opinion.

LARRY. So can you send it me? The data? I fly out very soon.

ANNOUNCER. All passengers – and that's all A-double-L – on Flight UA543 to Caracas. This is your final final call.

RACHEL. Me too. Okay, I'll have them email it to you.

LARRY. Or you could maybe send it now?

RACHEL *finds and forwards Caro's email to* LARRY, *as:*

RACHEL. Give me a minute.

ANNOUNCER. Okay, folks, this is now your last call for UA54 to beautiful Managua. Your crew awaits you eagerly at Gate Thirty-Five.

RACHEL. January data.

LARRY. Smartphone.

RACHEL. Yeah, it's cute.

LARRY. That's what the phone's called.

RACHEL. Yes, I know that. There, it's done. Now I must leave you.

LARRY (*looking at his phone*). Thanks. This'll turn it round.

RACHEL. You're very welcome. Bye.

ANNOUNCER. And, the remaining passengers remaining for Caracas, your flight really is now closing. Like, really.

RACHEL *turns back to him.*

RACHEL. What do you mean, 'turn it round'?

LARRY. Just what I said.

RACHEL. But they've got this stuff already. I'm just giving it to / you –

LARRY. 'They.'

Pause.

RACHEL. You are – you are working for President Bezborodko?

LARRY. Oh, did I say that?

Pause.

RACHEL. You shit.

LARRY *shrugs.*

You're working for the other side.

LARRY. Yup.

RACHEL. You *fuck.*

LARRY. Dishonour before death.

RACHEL. Give me your phone.

LARRY isn't going to do that. RACHEL grabs at his phone, he holds it away from her.

LARRY. Don't you think we owe it to these people to create conditions for a proper contest?

RACHEL. What, now you're a beacon of good democratic practice?

LARRY. I'm doing what I do.

He makes to go. RACHEL catches up with him and stands in his path.

RACHEL. And this is, what? For breaking up / the company –

LARRY. You could have fucking called.

Pause. The STEWARD arrives with RACHEL's hand luggage and duty-free bag. RACHEL stands.

RACHEL. Say again?

STEWARD. Mrs Moss?

LARRY. You heard.

RACHEL. What, Colorado? Moira? Breaking up the company?

LARRY. All three.

He makes to go. She follows him.

RACHEL. Larry, for Christ's sake, you're not serious.

LARRY. As you told me once before.

RACHEL. But still – this couldn't be. Larry, this couldn't be revenge.

LARRY. Try me.

He's going.

RACHEL (*calls*). So who's your fucking candidate?

LARRY. Why not fucking google it?

He's gone.

STEWARD. Mrs Moss?

RACHEL. Ms. Yes?

STEWARD. I'm sorry to harass you, but your flight for Caracas is actually closing. In the sense of, if you don't go now, your luggage will be flung onto the tarmac and you won't get on the plane. That's if you're still going to Caracas.

Pause.

RACHEL. Not any more.

Scene Fourteen

2010. The Angel of the Nation. PETR, *now fifty-one, enters with* AIDES, *including* OLEG, *now twenty-eight.* PETR *looks to* OLEG, *who straightens his tie.* PETR *goes to a microphone. He coughs, then:*

PETR (*Slavic language*). Sunarodnitsi. Az obiaviavam dnes kandidaturata si za president. [Fellow countrymen. Today I am announcing my candidacy for the presidency.]

Blackout.

End of Act One.

ACT TWO

'The economic crisis of 2008 had bred a deep distrust of business elites and the casino capitalism that, writ large, almost destroyed the world financial order... Confidence that the political economy of the West was a model for the future of mankind had been linked to the belief that Western elites knew what they were doing. Suddenly it was obvious that they didn't.'

Ivan Krastev and Stephen Holmes,
The Light That Failed: A Reckoning

'Elsewhere in Europe, national populists like Hungary's Viktor Orban argue that liberal politicians within the EU, along with the billionaire Hungarian-Jewish financier George Soros, are engaged in a plot to flood Hungary and "Christian" Europe with Muslim immigrants and refugees, which they see as part of a quest to dismantle Western nations and usher in a borderless world that is subservient to capitalism.'

Roger Eatwell and Matthew Goodwin, *National Populism: The Revolt Against Liberal Democracy*

'We went to teach them democracy, they taught us dictatorship.'

Ben Rhodes, former President Obama aide,
After the Fall: Being American in the World We've Made

Scene One

2009. JUSTIN, British, in his thirties. A PowerPoint presentation. JUSTIN's company is called Brand Your Land.

JUSTIN. Okay, imagine this. Everyone's a brand.

If they're not branding themself, then someone else is doing it for them.

Your brand is what they say about you when you leave the room.

As with a person, so with a country. Including yours.

Three basic principles.

Nothing's neutral. Everything's supporting your brand or undermining it. Your airport baggage lounge. The colour of your passport. The street names in your capital. The music in your hotel lounge.

Don't lie. Your brand must be a viable commodity. Do people really think 'The Norway of North Africa' is going to work for Libya?

But you can say something true by saying something new. Estonia: not Baltic, Nordic.

Well, they invented Skype. Who knew?

But accept the irony. Your country is distinct, unique. But everyone agrees about the six preferables:

(As if on the screen.) An efficient airline.

An attractive coastline

Bad luck, Hungary.

An appealing national cuisine.

Top tip: call it 'street food'.

Recognised as fair and just.

Gay-friendly.

And, naturally, sorry Scots –

Good weather.

So we asked people all across the world what they thought of you. And there's many positives. Skiing. Churches. Your famous song festival. Low-price alcohol. Beautiful women. But some of those positives are also negatives. Drunkenness and prostitution.

But the main problem is your past.

The rotting factories. The smokestack industries. The crumbling monuments.

Which brings us to my five dichotomies.

Traditional Transforming.

Strange Normal.

Closed Open.

Backward Forward.

Old and New.

And we had a go.

'Open for business.'

'This is what normal looks like.'

'Europe starts here.'

But finally, we think the best:

'At the heart of Europe. A land on song.'

Applause.

LARRY *appears with fairly rough luggage.*

LARRY. So where the hell am I?

The brand scene disappears.

Scene Two

2010. A workers' café. Early morning. A table. A young woman WAITER. *Popped-up folky music.* LARRY *has just been delivered here from his plane. He has been met here by* OLEG, *now twenty-eight, sitting at a table. On the table is a bottle and three glasses.*

OLEG. Ah, Mr Yeates.

LARRY. Yes.

The WAITER *goes out.* OLEG *shakes* LARRY*'s hand.*

OLEG. You have good flight?

LARRY. I have a long flight.

OLEG. Now you will like breakfast.

LARRY. Well, they gave me something / on the plane –

OLEG. A proper national breakfast, in the favourite restaurant of Candidate Lutsevic.

The WAITER *is bringing in a plate of sinister white food.*

LARRY (*looks around*). Oh, yeah?

OLEG. This is one reason he will meet you here. Have some fungal brandy.

LARRY (*looks at his watch*). Uh…

The WAITER *puts down the food.*

WAITER. It is our most famous national drink. Magic with Seven-Up.

LARRY *has a sip.*

LARRY. You don't say. And this is – ?

WAITER. It is cow stomach lining cooked with goose fat.

LARRY. Ah. You know…

WAITER. It is great national favourite also.

She goes and stands against the wall.

LARRY. Just like the music.

OLEG *signals the* WAITER *to turn off the music. She does so and returns to the same place, as:*

You're not eating?

OLEG. I breakfast at home.

LARRY. Smart move.

He tries a tiny bit. Poking at another bit.

What's this?

OLEG. The goose fat. In South Carolina, I once eat grits. Now, before the candidate arrive –

LARRY. – you tell me who you are.

OLEG. I am Oleg Sogolyev. I am adviser to Mr Petr Lutsevic, the leading opposition candidate in our upcoming presidential election. We hire you – on your own suggestion – to advise us how to strip the bark off President Liudmilla Bezborodko.

LARRY. Who was in charge when the economy went south. And said some ill-judged things at Davos and is slipping in the polls.

OLEG. Just so.

LARRY. And whose daughter tried to copyright the Sunflower Revolution?

OLEG. Natalia. And drive round Kosice in a big Merc as a consequence.

LARRY *takes out a notebook and writes.*

In fact, I meet her once in US university.

LARRY. What was she doing?

OLEG. Playing the trumpet. Falling in love.

LARRY. With you?

ACT TWO, SCENE TWO 71

OLEG. Your country. Free market, enterprise and I think free love. The national brand is her idea.

LARRY (*the breakfast*). A good idea?

OLEG. Well, we are told to build an Olympic velodrome and to enter the Eurovision Song Contest. They do not promote the stomach lining in the branding. They invent a 'national dish' you make with filo pastry.

LARRY. You ain't a fan.

OLEG. Nor we think are people who we need to vote for us.

A screech of brakes. OLEG *looks at his watch and stands.*

He's early.

LARRY. What?

Door slam.

OLEG. The candidate. This is usual, and most annoying. I must say quickly –

A BODYGUARD *in a black suit bursts in. He checks out the joint.*

WAITER (*Slavic language*). A vie koi ste? [And who are you?]

LARRY. Yes?

The BODYGUARD *heads for the kitchen.*

WAITER (*Slavic language*). Izvinete! Tam vlizaneto e zabraneno! [Excuse me! It's forbidden to go there!]

The BODYGUARD *goes into the kitchen, followed by the* WAITER.

OLEG. Your task: persuade him, A: there is a problem. And B: –

LARRY. That I'm the one to solve it.

The BODYGUARD *comes out of the kitchen, followed by the* WAITER, *as* PETR *enters.*

WAITER (*Slavic language*). Dovolen? Niama bombi? [Satisfied? No bombs?]

The BODYGUARD *shakes his head.*

PETR (*Slavic language*). Izlez. [Go out.]

The BODYGUARD *goes out. This pleases the* WAITER. LARRY *stands.*

(*Hand out.*) Mr Yeates, welcome to our country.

LARRY (*shakes*). It's a pleasure.

They sit.

PETR. Do you enjoy your breakfast?

LARRY. I'm told it's your favourite.

PETR. Sadly I come from a breakfast meeting at the Hyatt Regency. You meet Oleg?

LARRY. With pleasure.

PETR. Who advise me to hire foreign strategists when we do so well already in the polls.

LARRY. You've just declared your candidature. You should be riding high.

PETR. In the crash our GDP drop to the level of Zimbabwe. We open up to foreign investment, as instructed by your countrymen, and find we are open up to disinvestment too.

LARRY. Mr Lutsevic, I am gaining / the –

PETR. Therefore it is no surprise when people feel they have been three times occupied. First by the Germans, then the Russians, now by the Americans. I'm sorry, I interrupt you. You were gaining something.

LARRY. The impression you don't want me here.

Pause.

PETR. When I last ask you to support me – via the person now my opponent – you turn me down. Apparently there might be bad things done here seventy years ago.

LARRY. And why am I here now?

ACT TWO, SCENE TWO 73

PETR (*with a glance at* OLEG). Now we hear a rumour that your former partner Rachel Moss has volunteered to join the President's campaign.

LARRY. Well, has she now.

PETR. That's your former business partner, who skewers you.

LARRY. Yet I taught her everything she knows.

PETR. Her mother is arrested fighting against repression of Black people in your country.

LARRY. They are both most moral ladies.

PETR. And she takes on Leonid Zhudov, Dark Master, and she whips his ass.

LARRY. Well, so she claims.

PETR. Whilst you beat up a recently elected state assemblyman in Colorado.

LARRY. Richly deserved.

PETR. Explaining your surprising modest fee.

LARRY. Unless I win.

PETR. And it would be good to know the everything that you taught her. And what she might advise the President to do.

Pause.

LARRY. If the rumour's true, Mrs Moss will advise erecting billboards and encouraging lawn signs. She will propose that Mrs Bezborodko announces measures that are friendly to small businesses, particularly hospitality – tax breaks for outdoor cafés and the like – and that she blames the crash on the Americans.

PETR. Lawn signs?

LARRY. A placard stuck in the front lawn of a suburban home. But most importantly, Mrs Moss's sage advice will be that the campaign should not be framed as a referendum on Bezborodko's time in office – which she would lose – but as a choice between her and you.

PETR. Which she will win? Because I am a giraffe?

LARRY. Well, like many former dissidents you are perceived as looking down on people who did not dissent. You are also thought to be stiff and distant. I look forward to addressing these presentational matters urgently.

PETR. And how?

LARRY. You will make the electorate your friend. You will surround yourself with working folks engaged in honest labour. When not in your hard hat you'll be telling jokes and hugging baby bears. You'll hardly ever wear a jacket, and when you have to – press conferences and the like – you'll be prepared down to the last 'um' and 'ah'. It will be hard work and you won't enjoy it. And from now on, you'll confine yourself to attacking your opponent – who you'll refer to by her name not office – by repeating a simple message, over and over, until it makes you scream.

PETR. And what's that?

LARRY. I'll let you know.

Pause. PETR *sits.*

PETR. I have a joke.

LARRY. Please sock it to me.

PETR. My opponent has made communism popular. Which is what communism failed to do for fifty years.

LARRY. Great. But the other way around. Ms Bezborodko has achieved in five years what the communists failed to do in fifty. Make communism popular.

PETR. You think it's funnier that way?

LARRY. It *is* funnier that way.

Slight pause. OLEG *pours brandies.*

OLEG. Then shall we drink to that?

LARRY. This makes the food taste better?

PETR. No, but you drink two glasses, and who cares?

LARRY. Joke two.

He pushes the plate across to PETR.

Enjoy.

CARO *approaches.*

CARO. Rachel.

Scene Three

Hotel lobby. Perhaps some agreeable light classical music. CARO *is there.* RACHEL *has just entered with her luggage. Perhaps signage: 'A Land on Song'.* (*In the language of the country: Stranata si pee: Страната си пее* [*'The land is singing'*].

RACHEL. And the Prez is coming here to meet me?

CARO. Hopefully.

RACHEL. Hopefully?

CARO. She saw the television interview. They think you made it look as if you'd overthrown Novotsky single-handed. 'I go where I am needed' didn't go down too well. And you were pretty rude about the phones.

RACHEL. She does know about my unique insight into the strategies of the other side?

CARO. I reminded them about last time. And how you were completely crucial, then and now. I didn't say it was all about a grudge match with your former partner.

RACHEL. Which it's not.

CARO. Oh no?

RACHEL. I don't want my work undone.

CARO. Your work?

RACHEL. Our work undone.

CARO. No more do I.

A moment. They they embrace.

RACHEL. So you've been, pretty permanently…

CARO. I spent Christmas in the mountains above Stal'ko. Beautiful.

RACHEL. That's rust-belt country?

CARO. Sure, there's coal mines. Does that matter?

RACHEL. Christmas.

CARO. I ate a lot of pickled cabbage.

RACHEL. No I meant, Christmas, you weren't back home with Mom.

CARO. No, not this year.

RACHEL. Caro, please tell me you're not going native.

CARO. Why should I do that?

Slight pause.

RACHEL. Okay. We're seven points behind.

Enter NATALIA, *twenty-five and very well dressed.*

NATALIA. Good afternoon.

RACHEL. Good afternoon.

CARO (*standing*). This is Natalia / Bez–

NATALIA. Natalia Bezborodko.

RACHEL. We've met. You were human amplifying in October Square.

NATALIA. Now, Freedom Square.

RACHEL. So, is your mother / coming –

NATALIA. The President is not available.

RACHEL. I thought, I thought we had… May I ask why not?

NATALIA. She attends the committee which oversees our famous annual Festival of Song.

ACT TWO, SCENE THREE   77

RACHEL. Well, that's a shame. Because I'm very keen to apologise for an interview I gave which may have given a wholly false impression. Before outlining a strategy to win her re-election now.

NATALIA. Part of my job is to shield the President from bad political advice.

RACHEL. What, like shadowing the euro just before a global crash?

Slight pause.

NATALIA. Why don't you summarise your proposition.

RACHEL. My proposition.

NATALIA. Yes.

After a moment.

RACHEL. So why does Caro think the British Labour Party was out of power for eighteen years in the eighties and the nineties?

NATALIA. This is relevant?

RACHEL. Bear with me.

She sits.

CARO. Well, because its traditional base among industrial workers was in decline.

RACHEL. Equivalent to your rust-belt nostalgics.

CARO. While the growing classes were small businesses, what we call white-collar workers, people in IT…

RACHEL. Lattes and laptops, metro minigarchs…

CARO. Who wanted to get on in the world, and frankly thought Labour disapproved of them.

NATALIA. We too have such disapproving people.

RACHEL. But also?

CARO. Also?

RACHEL. There was a growing class of people – our humanist intelligensia, creative enterprise – who'd been to college and had picked up open, liberal, tolerant ideas, about personal behaviour, and maybe feminism and gay rights as well. Maybe you recognise such people too.

NATALIA *sits.*

NATALIA. You describe my social circle.

RACHEL. And Caro's focus groups among those people demonstrate there are an increasing number here who fit both those demographics. And would find that unusual cocktail – business friendly and social liberal – to their taste. A coalition which if I was to sum up in a single word it would be 'European'.

NATALIA. And that's your strategy? To target these?

RACHEL. You betcha.

NATALIA. Then we have no problem.

RACHEL. You have huge problems. The 2008 crash threw your country back to the early nineties. Your government is mired in allegations of corruption. There are the Davos tapes. You personally are mired in allegations of corruption.

NATALIA *stands.*

NATALIA. Well, I think now to be frank this maybe ends our / conversation –

CARO *makes to stand, but* RACHEL *gestures her not to.*

RACHEL. Which is why you cannot fight this race as a referendum on your mother's leadership.

NATALIA *gives a shrug and makes to go.*

That's if she wants to win this thing.

NATALIA *turns back.*

NATALIA. And the strategy we should pursue?

RACHEL. I will outline to the President at her earliest convenience.

NATALIA. Maybe you send this in an email.

RACHEL. Face to face. And once I have been officially contracted.

CARO. Um, you know that Rachel used to work with Larry / Yeates –

NATALIA. Yes. I believe he is headhunted by a man who many years before returned to me a trumpet.

CARO. Which is one – just one – of the unique attributes she brings.

NATALIA looks to RACHEL.

RACHEL. Right now, I imagine Larry will be encouraging Petr Lutsevic to speak in shorter sentences, to push everything he says around to a simple slogan, to call the President by her name not her office, to wear fluorescent jackets, make jokes, and hang out with cute furry animals.

NATALIA. Lutsevic does not do jokes.

RACHEL. Well, I bet you he will now.

Pause.

NATALIA. I fix the date. And if all goes fine, we issue you a contract.

RACHEL. Right. Fine.

RACHEL and CARO stand.

I hope the song festival goes well.

NATALIA. Don't knock it. It chooses our country's entry to the Eurovision Song Contest.

RACHEL (*look to* CARO). Um…

CARO. It's / a –

NATALIA. It's a pop-song competition on international television. Previously won by Estonia and Ukraine. Much easier than joining NATO or EU. Initially my mother thought it was not entirely serious for us.

RACHEL. And now?

NATALIA. As you know well, the President is always open to persuasion.

She goes out.

RACHEL. Result. I think.

CARO. Yeah, great.

RACHEL. What's wrong?

CARO. There's nothing wrong.

RACHEL. I've known you for nine years.

CARO. There was a woman, in the focus groups. It's the data that I sent you. She lives in a small town in the rust belt, near Zabosc. She felt there were two sorts of people now. People who could live anywhere – our urban aspirationals, latte and laptops – and people who still live in the somewhere they were born. Drinking beer and beetroot soup. And I guess I wonder what we feel about wooing minigarchs.

RACHEL. Creating a coalition that will do the job that we've been asked to do.

Pause.

CARO. Yuh. And, Larry doesn't have our data.

RACHEL (*after the slightest of pauses*). Right.

She makes to go.

(*Sudden thought.*). The European Song Contest.

CARO. Eurovision.

RACHEL. And the people at the song festival pick the country's entry?

CARO. No, it's a national public vote. Huge numbers.

RACHEL. And can people listen to the songs already?

CARO. Sure. They're all over YouTube.

RACHEL. Then we should find out what kind of people like which ones.

ACT TWO, SCENE FOUR   81

CARO. Which *songs*?

RACHEL. Now tell me if I've got this straight. It used to be, people told us what they knew – what they thought, what they bought. Volvo-driving white-wine drinkers ours, gun-owning churchy people theirs. But now we're interested in stuff they don't know they're telling us, which we get from what they 'like'. Click Louis Vuitton and you're pro-choice, click hot tubs and you want to join the European Union. And Facebook knows you're pregnant before you do. And so why the songs? Because what they'll tell us is not what people think or buy but what they are.

CARO. And do we like that?

RACHEL. Do we have to like it?

Pause.

CARO. You. Social media.

RACHEL. Indulge me. Just two questions. Test the songs.

Scene Four

2010. RACHEL stands. We're now in a room in the Presidential Office. LIUDMILLA enters, followed by NATALIA, who carries the presidential iPad.

RACHEL. Madam President.

LIUDMILLA. Yes.

RACHEL. Before we start, I must apologise for seriously misspeaking in an interview I gave on US television.

LIUDMILLA. Oh?

RACHEL. And ill-thought opinions I expressed about your candidature during the previous campaign.

LIUDMILLA. You did?

RACHEL. Uh – yes?

LIUDMILLA. I don't remember.

RACHEL *throws a look to* NATALIA, *who doesn't respond.*

And now, your proposal.

She turns to NATALIA, *who hands her her iPad.*

RACHEL. Yes.

LIUDMILLA. You recommend a strategy which can be summed up as: reunite the Sunflower Coalition.

RACHEL. Yes.

NATALIA. Transforming. Normal. Open.

LIUDMILLA *(flipping through the document on the iPad)*. So. 'Widen recruitment to the Supreme Court.' Yes.

(*With a glance to* NATALIA.) 'Ease immigration rules.' Yes but with caveats.

RACHEL. Modern. International. Diverse.

NATALIA. And economic growth.

LIUDMILLA. 'Stop subsidising mines and bankrupt industries. Reduce tax for hospitality and IT start-ups.' Certainly. I see you mind less about Mrs Thatcher.

RACHEL *gives a confirming but 'so-so' gesture.*

(*Next.*) 'Gay couples adopt children.' Not Mrs T I think.

RACHEL. Exactly.

LIUDMILLA (*with a glance at* NATALIA). Then yes. 'End all legal restrictions on the sale of Sunflower Revolution merchandise.'

She looks at her daughter, who shrugs.

'Ease abortion laws. Start subsidising windmills. Forge closer ties to the European Union. Actually build the National Theatre.' Yes done done yes.

She hands the iPad back to NATALIA.

ACT TWO, SCENE FOUR 83

And all this to make my voters feel good about themselves. So successful in Wisconsin.

RACHEL (*pleased*). Yes. Now I recommend that we meet / weekly –

LIUDMILLA. I am fighting former ally. Who pledges solemnly he will never run against me. And you of course fight a former ally too.

RACHEL. Larry Yeates does not do pledges.

LIUDMILLA. And you fly round the world to shish-kebab his tail. How does that feel?

RACHEL. Good if we win.

LIUDMILLA. And presumably you know some things about him? Was there not a fight and a divorce?

Slight pause.

RACHEL. Not connected. And I wouldn't use it if it was.

(*Her practised line.*) I am here because I do not want to see our work undone.

LIUDMILLA. By Larry Yeates?

RACHEL. By anyone.

Slight pause.

LIUDMILLA. Of course. You will attend our Festival of Song?

RACHEL. Try and stop me.

LIUDMILLA. And still you think this cannot be a referendum on my presidency.

RACHEL. Davos. The crash. Shadowing the euro.

LIUDMILLA. The adviser has been fired.

NATALIA. He should have been arrested.

RACHEL. But if it's a choice between you and Petr Lutsevic, then you win.

LIUDMILLA. And this is what Larry Yeates would say?

RACHEL. It's what I say.

LIUDMILLA *smiles. Then:*

LIUDMILLA. Speaking of Lutsevic, he is this morning being most ridiculous. He makes a big speech in a field. Surrounded by the toilers of the world. In shirtsleeves. In this weather.

NATALIA. He asks 'Where must we go?' and answers 'Forwards and not backwards.'

LIUDMILLA. He goes forward actually to die of frostbite. And to plant a tree. Then he says: 'Mrs Bezborodko has made communism popular. Which communists did not succeed to do in fifty years.'

NATALIA. We think that is a joke.

RACHEL. That's Larry.

LIUDMILLA. But he puts his punchline first.

RACHEL. That'll be the candidate. No animals?

LIUDMILLA. Odd you say that. He strokes a cow.

She smiles and hands the iPad back to NATALIA.

(*As she sweeps out.*) I'm not sure why this meeting was so tricky to arrange.

She has gone.

NATALIA. Forgiven.

Scene Five

2010. PETR *is rehearsing a press conference. His notes are on the lectern. He grasps it tightly.*

PETR. First of all, let me say I am very grateful to the gentleman from CNN for his question. Of course it is good to make tax cuts for small businesses in my country. But in view of the overall national economic catastrophe –

LARRY *and* OLEG *have appeared. It's a rehearsal.*

LARRY. Okay, stop. Don't fuck the lectern. You look like you've a poker up your ass.

PETR *sighs. This has been going on a while.*

OLEG (*Slavic language*). Imate bezzhichen mikrofon, mozhete da se porazkhodite. [You've got a lapel mic. You can walk around.]

(*To* LARRY.) Lapel mic, he can move around.

PETR. Alright. First of all, may I thank the gentleman –

LARRY. Address the questioner by name. Don't thank him for the question, it looks like you're trying to work out what to say. If you do need time to work out what to say, use one of your transitional phrases.

PETR. Remind me.

OLEG. 'The bottom line.' 'What's important here...'

LARRY. 'I think what people really care about is...'

PETR (*Slavic language*). Iskate li da chuete otgovora? [Do you want to hear the answer?]

LARRY. Say again?

OLEG. Do we want to hear the answer?

LARRY. I want to hear him connect the answer to the message.

OLEG (*prompting, Slavic language*). Napred. Ne nazad! [Forwards not backwards.]

PETR. I am committed that I will take the country forward, yet again?

LARRY. Not backwards, to...

PETR. To?

OLEG (*Slavic language, prompting*). Koshmara na devedesette. [The nightmare of the nineties.]

PETR. Not backwards to –

LARRY. Don't fuck the *lectern* –

PETR. To the nightmare of the nineties, which is where the President –

LARRY. Mrs Bezborodko –

PETR. Would take us.

LARRY. *Is* –

PETR. Is take us. Taking us.

LARRY. *Yes*.

OLEG claps.

But remember that you won't have time to think.

OLEG. But still.

LARRY. Now something more aggressive.

OLEG. *More* aggressive?

PETR. I need a piss.

He walks out.

LARRY (*calls after him*). No comfort breaks in the real thing!

PETR (*calls as he goes*). This is not the real thing!

He's gone.

OLEG. Larry, there is no need to chew his ass. He does well.

LARRY. Not in the polls. Down another one-point-five.

OLEG. And this is necessary?

LARRY. It's essential.

LARRY looks beadily at OLEG, *then he sees* PETR *returning.*

LARRY. Kick his butt.

PETR *hadn't needed to pee, he'd needed to breathe.*

OLEG. That's quick.

PETR. As you say, no breaks in the real thing.

He goes back to the lectern.

So. Aggress me.

OLEG *flashes a look at* PETR. *Then:*

OLEG. Since six years now you withdraw from the presidential race in favour of Mrs Bezborodko. You pledge you will never run against her.

PETR. I do not think I said / 'never'.

OLEG. If she is better than you then, why run against her now?

PETR. I did not know then the answer to your question.

OLEG. Then answer it.

PETR. For all her promises, she takes the country backwards and not forwards.

OLEG. That is just a slogan.

PETR *flashes a look at* LARRY; *he agrees. But then:*

PETR. I did not expect that she will focus on reproductive rights or closing mines or reinventing national costume or throwing wide our borders to the world. But what people really want / to hear about –

LARRY. And then how d'you turn the country round?

PETR. I say, I take it forward –

OLEG. Be specific!

PETR. I don't want old ladies have to sell their / dinner –

OLEG. When did you last see an old lady / selling –

PETR. I ask, who Mrs Bezborodko's tax cut and free choices will / leave out.

OLEG. That doesn't answer, what you do.

PETR. I say, 'I increase pensions.'

OLEG. And?

PETR. And protect our industries / from –

LARRY. What did you say?

Slight pause.

PETR. I increase pensions and protect / our –

LARRY. Before that.

PETR. I – um…

OLEG. He asks what open borders and free markets and abortion will leave out.

LARRY. No, he didn't. He asked *who* it leaves out.

PETR. Yes? Is that / wrong?

LARRY. Who do those policies leave out? What sort of people? Does it leave out you?

PETR. Me?

LARRY. Or the folks you came from.

Pause.

PETR. I am spoken about often as a well-off liberal person. Someone who suffers much in the days of communism but now is doing pretty nicely thank you. 'Davos dissident.' But the people who I come from do not do so much nicely thank you. And I cannot tie my tie or speak with proper grammar and I want to change things for the better.

LARRY. Snap.

PETR. Snap?

LARRY. I come from Flint, in Michigan. Blue-collar Catholic family. We used to make automobiles. Not any more.

Slight pause.

Me too.

OLEG. And the question?

PETR. So, yes, as we move off – forward, towards our radiant European future –

LARRY. Forgive me.

PETR. What?

LARRY. Just a moment.

He gets out his phone and finds something on it. This takes a little time. PETR *and* OLEG *look at each other. A bit of a shrug between them. Eventually:*

PETR (*Slavic language*). Kakvo stava? [What is going on?]

OLEG (*Slavic language*). Niamam si napredstava. [I have no idea.]

PETR. Well, perhaps now, I do take my / piss –

LARRY. Yes.

(*To* PETR *and* OLEG.) I'm sorry. There was a woman, in a focus group. And she talked about falling pensions and no jobs, but then she goes off on this riff about two different sorts of people, what she called the somewhere people, living where they came from, what apparently they call 'rust-belt nostalgics' and/or 'beer'n'borscht' –

OLEG. We should use / that.

LARRY. – and the anywheres who come to the cities and drink lattes and use laptops and change jobs every other Friday and feel they are the future.

OLEG (*good*). Somewhere, anywhere.

LARRY (*putting his phone away*). And she said, she didn't think this was her country any more.

Pause.

What my opponent's done is to build a new coalition for her candidate. Free market and free love. You could say, rum and tonic. But by doing so she's also built an opposing coalition on our side. Which believes in state aid for their industries and pensions for the old folks, just like our Democrats back home. But unlike the Democrats they're also sold on traditional family values and the guarding of our borders. And they've left the gin and Coke for us.

PETR (*Slavic language*). Kakvi gi govori? [What's he talking about?]

OLEG (*Slavic language*). Kokteili. [Cocktails.]

LARRY. But most important, it's not just a different set of policies. It's a different set of people. Who I think could win us the election.

OLEG. And they haven't spotted that?

LARRY. I don't think so.

PETR. Why not?

LARRY. Because if they had they'd not be doing what they're doing now.

Scene Six

2010. The Festival of Song. A VIP area, cordoned off with velvet ropes. Canapés and drinks on a trestle table. RACHEL *and* CARO *are waiting. Like everyone except* CARO, RACHEL *is wearing Eurovision kit: feather boas, deely bopper headbands.* LIUDMILLA, NATALIA *and* JUSTIN *appear.*

LIUDMILLA. Rachel. I gather we're flatlining.

RACHEL. You have stabilised.

LIUDMILLA. Justin, meet Team Bezborodko. Justin brands us.

JUSTIN. Justin made some helpful suggestions.

RACHEL. The six preferables.

NATALIA. Does anyone want pink fizz?

ACT TWO, SCENE SIX

NATALIA is pouring fizz for JUSTIN and her mother. She gestures to RACHEL and CARO. RACHEL would like some, CARO not.

LIUDMILLA. And now he consults for us on Eurovision.

NATALIA. We love the Sunflower song.

LIUDMILLA. Obviously.

NATALIA *(sings a snatch).*
Hey! Hey! Hey!

RACHEL. Yes, in fact, / we –

JUSTIN. I like Christina. 'How-De-Do-Di'.

RACHEL. As do seventeen-point-five per cent of your current definites.

JUSTIN *(sings).*
How-di-something, la-la-la…

NATALIA *(corrects).*
– la-*di*-la –

LIUDMILLA. Say again?

RACHEL nods to CARO.

CARO. We've tested all the songs.

NATALIA. Tested?

CARO. On representative segments of the population.

NATALIA. There is no point in that.

LIUDMILLA. You cannot vote for the song of your own country.

RACHEL. That isn't why we did it.

She nods to CARO, who gets out her phone.

LIUDMILLA. Then why…?

JUSTIN. I imagine Rachel would like to find out what kind of people like what kind of song.

LIUDMILLA. And I hope she asks also what they plan to vote in the election.

RACHEL. Of course. We asked two questions.

LIUDMILLA. And what do you discover?

RACHEL. Well, predictably, 'Roar' by – ?

CARO. Vroom.

JUSTIN (*sings*).
   One! Two! Three! Four!

   Maybe others join, not in a good way.

   They sing, we ROAR.

RACHEL. Is favourite with beer'n'borscht.

NATALIA. Surprise surprise.

CARO. Young men. Frequent visitors to the US Marine Corps. Arsenal.

NATALIA. And slurping.

JUSTIN (*explains*). Football hooligans.

LIUDMILLA. Brawling and tattoos. And Rodina?

CARO. Which we translate as 'Homeland', and their song as 'Our Mountains Are Our Dreams'. The people who favour this song most strongly are great patriotic warriors and rust-belt nostalgics.

NATALIA. And rust-belt racialists no doubt. 'Faith family and flags.'

LIUDMILLA. And nostalgia for foreign occupation.

CARO. And they like four-wheel drives, oddly some vegan sites, Red Army Choir, and churches. And yes, concerns about migration.

NATALIA. All these non-existent immigrating people visiting their invisible mosques.

JUSTIN. And Christina?

RACHEL. Two-job suburbanites with kids?

CARO. Topshop, Katy Perry.

LIUDMILLA. And I am presuming Sunflower people are our people.

CARO. Yes, but –

JUSTIN. The song now in English with new lyrics.

NATALIA. 'But'?

CARO. But I wonder if we should be doing this.

Pause.

NATALIA. Doing what?

CARO. Using a song contest for political purposes.

NATALIA. You think that Eurovision is primarily a song contest?

CARO. Isn't it?

LIUDMILLA. Justin, what do you think of this in your opinion?

They turn to JUSTIN *as* NATALIA *does refills.*

NATALIA. He's encyclopaedic.

JUSTIN. Well, of course, the contest was conceived as a weapon in the Cold War.

RACHEL. Naturally, all our fault.

JUSTIN. The West: fun, pop, with it, up to date. Eastern Europe: staid and dull. Thus, not surprisingly, when the Berlin Wall came down, entering or even better winning Eurovision was a passport to the West.

NATALIA. Serbia, Estonia. Ukraine.

(*Filling up* JUSTIN*'s glass, and prompting.*) And of course the contest is quite prone to political and cultural controversy. Particularly related to LGBT issues.

JUSTIN. Well, Ireland first wins in 1970, with a lovely Derry Catholic girl called Dana. Twenty-eight years later, Israel's entry is a transsexual called Dana International, whose winning entry is a song called 'Diva'.

NATALIA. Which causes outrage among Israeli Orthodox and some people dismiss as pinkwashing.

RACHEL. Say again?

JUSTIN. Israel showing how open and tolerant they are.

NATALIA. Compared to the Muslim countries which surround them.

LIUDMILLA. Which is true, obviously. And when Russia hosts, the opening song is by a so-called lesbian duo called Tatu, in front of a pink tank.

NATALIA. While a gay pride demonstration is broken up outside.

JUSTIN. So what appears to be a music contest is in fact a rite of passage for emerging democracies, a nation brander, a battleground in the culture war, or a crusade for human rights. What's hard to argue is that it's a way of picking the best pop song in Europe.

Laughter.

CARO. But, as you say, it could also be seen as the West telling the rest how to live their lives. Again.

Pause.

NATALIA. Well, in this case, the West says good things, surely.

CARO. What, that you can't wear a veil and be a European? Or to be a citizen you can't believe in faith and flag?

NATALIA. Except I think the 'faith flag' people are not so keen on Muslims actually.

CARO. No.

NATALIA. Well, no gays, no choice, no foreigners. I call intolerance.

Pause.

LIUDMILLA. I think now is the second half. Justin.

JUSTIN. What was the second question?

Slight pause.

You said you asked two questions.

RACHEL. Well, we asked / who –

JUSTIN. Let me guess. Having asked what song they liked most, you asked which they liked least.

RACHEL (*pleased*). Yup.

(*Prompting.*) Caro.

CARO *consults her iPad.*

CARO. Well, it's what you would expect. Their base, which goes for Rodina and Clickbait...

NATALIA. Vroom.

CARO. For sure, they don't like Sunshine. Nor 'How-De-Do-Di', actually.

JUSTIN. Mixed bag.

LIUDMILLA. And our targets? Suburbanites with kids? The precarious middle?

CARO. Well, what they like is varied. Sunshine, Christina –

NATALIA. Mixed bag again.

JUSTIN. What they don't like?

CARO. Vroom.

NATALIA. Who doesn't?

RACHEL. None of them.

Slight pause.

LIUDMILLA. And people tend to vote for what makes them feel good about themselves. And against, what doesn't. Rachel's Law.

NATALIA. And who likes Vroom? Caro?

CARO. Well, as you put it, football hooligans and racists with tattoos.

LIUDMILLA. Then we make clear to the people who we want we are not Vroom people. And they're not either.

RACHEL. Yes.

CARO. Or no.

NATALIA. Why 'no'?

Everyone looks at CARO.

CARO. So here's the thing. I like to ask people what they think and sometimes what they feel. I'm not so keen on harvesting their wants and likes, for other things, for clothes and cars and songs, so we clever people can work out how to make them want the things they don't want but we want them to.

NATALIA. Like, who to vote for.

CARO. Yes. I'm not so sure that's really – ethical.

Pause.

LIUDMILLA. All right. You come here to help a country turn from a dictatorship into a liberal democracy. And maybe some people sneer at that. And maybe you are a little patronising and smug, and perhaps I say so. But actually, if you are that country, I'd say that it's a very ethical endeavour.

JUSTIN. Heroic, even.

LIUDMILLA. Actually.

NATALIA. Hear hear.

JUSTIN. In 1974, the Portuguese entry was called 'E Depois do Adeus', 'Afterwards, Goodbye'. And its being played on national radio was the signal for the Carnation Revolution, which overthrew fascism. Just saying.

JUSTIN knocks back his champagne and follows LIUDMILLA out.

RACHEL. So what the fuck was that about?

CARO. I'm sneering?

RACHEL. No of course not.

CARO. It's just – I think sometimes, yes, we can be a little smug. About people who have the temerity not to agree with us.

NATALIA. Well, this is so very strange.

CARO. Oh, why?

NATALIA. Coming from a noted liberal. Even vegetarian.

CARO. Vegan. Lesbian. But from Rotherham.

RACHEL. British rust belt.

NATALIA. Where no doubt they are not so much politically correct.

CARO. No, and isn't that convenient.

NATALIA. Convenient?

CARO. That all these poor people who we thought we should support because they were heroic workers, now we find they're actually backward, stupid and reactionary, they're homophobes and racists –

NATALIA. And are they *not* / homophobic –

CARO. And so thank goodness we don't need to support them or to listen to them any more. And is that so ethical? Like, really?

RACHEL. Caro.

NATALIA. And in Rotherham, maybe, they all wear tattoos?

CARO. And I've been thinking. You've got the data. There's great people on the ground. Maybe my work's done here.

NATALIA. You're quitting?

CARO. You see, my mother has tattoos.

NATALIA. Well, we have to just muddle on without you, Caroline.

She goes out. Pause.

RACHEL. Caro, don't quit.

CARO. I said. I think I'm done.

RACHEL. Is it something in the groups? The focus groups you went back to, for the songs?

CARO. It's what I said.

RACHEL. Is this why you spent Christmas halfway up a mountain eating cabbage two thousand miles from home?

CARO. You know, I saw this coming.

RACHEL. How?

CARO. A focus group in Bolton. Last year. Voter One would renationalise the water companies and banks and pharmaceuticals and make us all more equal.

RACHEL. Labour.

CARO. And Voter Two: 'You know what gets my goat? You can't call Christmas Christmas any more. You say "too many immigrants" and you're racist, it's all "put gay rights first and nobody can be a normal family".'

RACHEL. And, presumably / that's –

CARO. And what do they have in common? These two people?

RACHEL doesn't know what CARO's driving at.

They were actually one person. And it's these people Larry's going for. And we're letting him because we think these people are deplorable.

RACHEL. I think their opinions are deplorable.

CARO. No you don't. It isn't what they think, that gets to you. It's what they are.

Enter LARRY, dressed in a towel.

LARRY. Oh. Can I help you?

Scene Seven

2010. The changing room of a hotel sauna/steam room. CARO *is dressed as she was in the previous scene, but now with a big suitcase.* LARRY *stands there, in his towel.*

CARO. I'm not doing this.

LARRY. Okay?

CARO. This isn't happening.

LARRY. It's not?

CARO. This is the last thing that I want to do…

LARRY. So, uh…

CARO. I'm Caro Wheeler. Maybe you remember –

LARRY. Sure, we met in Illinois.

CARO. I'm headed for the airport.

LARRY. Right. Do you want for me to call / you a –

CARO. So here's the thing.

LARRY. What thing?

CARO *breathes deeply, takes out a document of half a dozen pages.*

CARO. I can't give you this. You've never read it. You've got one minute. If you get it, then you get it. If you don't, bye-bye.

A moment, then she thrusts the document at LARRY.
LARRY *flips for a moment or two.*

LARRY. So I'm guessing that you've found the vortex.

CARO. You've got thirty seconds.

LARRY. It's not immigration.

CARO. No, it's not, you got it wrong, so hand it back.

LARRY (*spotting in the document*). It's not just the people coming in. It's the people they're replacing.

Pause.

CARO. Yup. You got it.

He hands it back.

LARRY. I'd got it already.

CARO. Had you?

(*Making to go.*) Then I –

LARRY. But you could still tell me how you got it.

He sits on a bench.

So what's the accent? Liverpool?

CARO. Yorkshire. British rust belt. What Margaret Thatcher left of it.

LARRY. I'm from Flint. What Reagan but also Clinton left of upstate Michigan.

CARO. I did some groups some months ago. Former industrial, what we call rust-belt nostalgics. We discussed their considerable economic woes.

LARRY. As you would.

CARO. And we also found there were lots of social things that bothered them: abortion, divorce, homosexuality. City things.

LARRY. Latte and laptop people.

CARO. But nothing more important than the economic issues.

LARRY. They weren't salient.

CARO. Not salient enough. And of course since then I've been concentrating on our waverers. But recently I went back to see my people in the rust belt.

LARRY. Same people?

CARO. Mostly. And I asked them about pop songs.

LARRY. Eurothing.

CARO. But I also asked them what I asked them last time. And it was different. Something had happened. It wasn't jobs and pensions any more.

LARRY. It was all –

CARO. It was all the young people leaving. Leaving their villages, leaving the country. Going to the cities, or the West, and either never coming back or coming back with new ideas about their right to live their lives the way they want. Gay rights. Abortion. And as my people's places emptied, there would be other people coming in to sweep the streets and fill the cars with petrol and serve coffee. And as they come from anywhere they don't know anything about the places where these people live. The places and their pasts. And abortion and gay rights and divorce and immigration and above all emigration are suddenly all wrapped up in the same package, and it's just a process which they never voted for. And then they start asking, who's to blame, who wants all this to happen, for them to be replaced. And their country's not their country any more.

LARRY. The vortex.

LARRY changes into day clothes.

CARO. And I don't agree with them, of course. But I think like anyone they deserve to have a voice.

LARRY. 'My people.'

CARO. Did I say that?

LARRY. 'My people in the rust belt.' Yes.

CARO. Well, I obviously can't wish you luck.

LARRY. Nor me. But have a great trip home.

CARO (*turning to go*). Well, ta.

LARRY. One thing. Do they say who the people are, who want all this?

CARO. Some people say, they're a kind of elite.

LARRY. What kind?

CARO. Urban. Liberal.

LARRY. Lattes and laptops.

LARRY. And no one else?

CARO. Well, I guess the businessmen who import foreign workers.

LARRY. And that's all?

CARO. One woman said, she sometimes thinks, the people doing all of this don't seem to come from any place at all.

Slight pause.

But I don't think they really know.

LARRY *comes out of the cubicle, and sits to put on his shoes and socks.* CARO *realises something.*

LARRY. Maybe they should.

CARO. Where did you get that?

LARRY. What?

CARO. 'Latte and Laptop.' As a term we use.

LARRY. Wasn't it in the TV interview? Along with 'rust-belt / nostalgics' –

CARO. No it wasn't. It was in…

LARRY *looks up at her. She realises.*

You saw the January data. She shared the fucking data.

LARRY *stands, puts on his jacket.*

LARRY. So did you.

CARO. 'It was in the TV interview.' And I've just – fuck it – I've just trusted you.

LARRY. You did.

CARO *gets it.*

CARO. You hadn't got it.

LARRY. What?

CARO. Replacement, as the vortex. You hadn't got it, till I showed you.

LARRY. Got it now.

They look at each other. Then LARRY *turns away.*

Scene Eight

2010. Eurovision. PETR, OLEG *and* LARRY *are watching Sunshine singing their song.*

SUNSHINE.
We are the future,
The future is here.
A future of rainbows,
A world without fear.

Imagine a future, freed from the past
Farewell to envy and hatred at last.
The Sunflower people follow the call:
Throw open the border and tear down the wall.

Chorus:
Sunshine – yours, mine
Darkness is no more
Rainbows will lead us
To a brighter shore
The future is here!

We're living our lives and we're sharing our songs
No nations or races, they've lasted too long.
If we open our hearts, then guess what we'll find:
There's only one race and that's humankind.

Chorus.

Born a man or a woman, we're both and we're none
In the world we are many, in our hearts we are one.

We are what we feel and for that we will fight
Whoever we love, then we have the right.
We must have the right!

Scene Nine

PETR, LARRY *and* OLEG. PETR *has an English copy of the script* LARRY *and* OLEG *have written for him.* PETR *goes through the speech, making comments and amendments. This wasn't what* LARRY *or* OLEG *expected.*

PETR (*making the amendments*). 'So do we need a costly jamboree, mocking our traditional values?' I'm going to say – (*Slavic language.*) Nashite traditsionni khristiianski tsennosti. [Our traditional Christian values.]

OLEG. 'Our traditional Christian values.' You mean...

PETR. You know what I mean. 'Do we really need our nation branded by another country?' Maybe, 'foreign'.

LARRY. Worth trying. Now –

PETR. 'But the question is: who is behind the branders and the mockers? It is a liberal elite.' Very good.

LARRY. Well, thanks.

PETR. 'But perhaps there are people who lurk behind the people. Who operate in secret, in the shadows.'

LARRY. Uh – I don't remember that.

PETR. No, this is new. I write it down for you.

PETR *waves a scrap of paper.* LARRY *looks to* OLEG.

LARRY. What?

OLEG *goes to look at the paper, but* PETR *hands it to* LARRY.

PETR. I write for you in English.

LARRY *looks at the paper, then hands it to* OLEG.

LARRY. What do you think?

OLEG. I would not suggest this.

LARRY. Nor would I.

PETR. Happily you have a candidate who wants to win this thing.

He takes back the paper.

I like what you say about the people who seem to come from no real place at all. And now I take my piss.

He goes out.

LARRY. And do you think. If he said that, in this country, now…?

OLEG. I suppose… He does not actually say it.

LARRY. Does he need to?

PETR *delivering his speech.*

PETR (*Slavic language*). Mozhe bi ima khora koito operirat taino, v siankite. [But perhaps there are people who lurk behind the people, who operate in secret, in the shadows.]

Scene Ten

Campaign room. NATALIA, LIUDMILLA *and* RACHEL *and maybe* OTHER AIDES *are watching the broadcast of* PETR*'s speech, delivered in front of the Angel of the Nation. He is dressed in a fine suit, his tie neatly tied and surrounded by* POLICEMEN, SOLDIERS *and* WORKERS *with national flags.*

PETR (*Slavic language*). V chii interes e da se potupkvat nashite narodni tsennosti? [Whose interests it is in, to trample our country's values?]

NATALIA. Whose interests is it, to trample on our country's values.

PETR (*Slavic language*). Agentite na evropeiskiia suiuz koito iskat da otvoriat granitsite ni kum Muhamedanski prishultsi. [The agents of the European Union, who want to open up our borders to the Islamic aliens.]

LIUDMILLA. The agents of the EU, who want to throw our borders open to the Islamic hordes.

PETR (*Slavic language*). Finansovata klasa – koiato sponsorira Schaefer Educational Foundation, i natiska nashite mladi momicheta da se oburnat kum perverzii i da se otkazhat ot maichinstvoto. [The financier class, the citizens of nowhere, who sponsor the Schaefer Educational Foundation, and promote perversion and spurn motherhood.]

LIUDMILLA. The financiers and speculators who are citizens of nowhere. Who control the Schaefer Educational Foundation, who promote perversion and spurn motherhood.

RACHEL. Holy shit.

PETR (*Slavic language*). Ne samo liberalnite eliti v medii, universiteti, no I globalistite elit koito gi kontrolirat. Tezi khora iskat da izcheznem, da ni iztriiat I zameniat s drugi. [Not just the liberal elites in the media and universities, but the rootless globalists who pull their strings. These people who want us to disappear, to erase us and replace our people with another.]

ACT TWO, SCENE TEN   107

LIUDMILLA. Not just the liberal elites in the media and universities, but the rootless globalists who pull their strings. Who want to erase us, and replace our people with another.

PETR (*Slavic language*). Obrushtam se kum vsichki koito kazvat, che Evropa e nasheto budeshte. Tova veche ne e istinata. Nie sme budheshteto na Evropa. [I turn to the people who say that our future is Europe, I say that is no longer true. We are now Europe's future.]

LIUDMILLA. To the people who say that our future is Europe, I say that is no longer true.

RACHEL. 'We are Europe's future now'?

LIUDMILLA. We are Europe's future now.

Huge applause. NATALIA *freezes the image on the screen.*

NATALIA. What is he doing?

LIUDMILLA. What he is doing. Who is Schaefer?

NATALIA. He runs a charity.

LIUDMILLA. What else? Rachel?

RACHEL. He is a billionaire.

LIUDMILLA. And what else?

Slight pause.

NATALIA. We must respond to this.

She makes a phone call.

LIUDMILLA. A 'rootless globalist'. A puppeteer. And this from your former colleague. Playing this card. In this country. With its history. He doesn't even have to say the word.

NATALIA (*her call answered, Slavic language*). Vidia li go? [So did you see it?]

RACHEL. I don't... I can't believe that this could still swing an election, in this country, now.

NATALIA (*phone, Slavic language*). Shte pitam kolko vreme I triabva. [I'll ask how long she needs.]

LIUDMILLA. Oh, no? Then it proves how little you have understood about small family businesses and precarious professionals. In this kind of country. Not to mention the rural dispossessed. And Vroom.

(*To* NATALIA. *Slavic language.*) Triiset minuti. Izvikai Sergei Kolorenko. [Thirty minutes. Get Sergei Kolorenko.]

NATALIA (*phone. Slavic language*). Polovin chas. Izvikai Sergei. [She says half an hour. Get Sergei.]

RACHEL. Look, what I would advise / is that –

LIUDMILLA. No, we have had enough advice.

NATALIA (*phone, Slavic language*). Doskoro. [Till soon.]

NATALIA *ends her call.*

(*To* LIUDMILLA.) Pres-conferentsiia sled polovin chas. [Press conference in half an hour.]

LIUDMILLA. You people. Coming here, to tell us how to do democracy. The demon you've unleashed.

RACHEL. I still – I can't believe that Larry wrote that.

LIUDMILLA. Oh, no? 'Lesbians for Franklyn'.

She goes out. NATALIA *bleakly looks at* RACHEL.

RACHEL. I missed it.

NATALIA. What?

RACHEL. Caro spotted it. But she didn't spot that it was my idea.

NATALIA*'s phone goes. She answers.*

NATALIA (*Slavic language*). Alo? [Hallo?]

Slight pause.

Tia idva sega. [She's on her way.]

RACHEL. Why should we assume that if people think this, they think that? Why shouldn't they fix their cocktail any way they damn well like? And we serve our cocktail. And he serves his. And blames everything that's wrong on a conspiracy of Jewish masterminds, as imagined by the Tsarist secret police, all those years ago.

NATALIA. We are too polite about those who oppose us and what they think. We are ashamed, because they are impoverished. Of course, they shouldn't be. Maybe, yes, it was more shock than therapy. But what they say is wrong. We should be open, forward. It is right that you can love the people that you want to. It is the wildest paranoia that these opinions are a plot by international bankers to replace our population. It is good to be in Europe with other European people, facing outward to the world. It is better to have open doors to refugees who are being killed in Afghanistan and starved in Africa. These are the opinions of good people, kind, decent people. Even if the people who do not agree are miserable and poor.

RACHEL. Look. This can / be fixed –

NATALIA. And now I'm sorry, we have work to do. If we want to save this thing.

NATALIA goes out. Enter ZHUDOV, with a hunting rifle.

ZHUDOV. Mr Larry Yeates?

RACHEL *goes.*

Scene Eleven

2014. Summer. The Presidential Palace. A long table.
ZHUDOV *sits at one end of the table,* LARRY *at the other.*
ZHUDOV *places the rifle on the table.*

LARRY. Correct. And who are you?

ZHUDOV. I am Leonid Zhudov. Welcome to the Presidential Palace. I trust you you are suitably appalled by the gross display of ostentatious kitsch which now surrounds you.

They shake hands.

LARRY. And this is all / the current –

ZHUDOV. Which we all blame naturally on the presidential predecessor, Liudmilla Bezborodko. Even the gun.

LARRY. The gun.

ZHUDOV. Apparently a gift from Her Majesty the Queen.

(*Holding up the rifle.*) Would you like to kill some animals?

LARRY (*with a shake of his head*). You're back.

ZHUDOV. I go wherever my government deems it valuable for me to be.

ZHUDOV *smiles and puts down the rifle. He gestures to* LARRY *to sit. They both do.*

How is your flight?

LARRY. The national airline's first-class offer has improved.

ZHUDOV. I will inform the President.

LARRY. I'd assumed that I was here to discuss the campaign for his re-election.

ZHUDOV. Not exactly. And, of course, he's very busy.

LARRY (*short, a little angry*). So I understand. For example, busy banning independent civil bodies in receipt of foreign aid.

ZHUDOV. Requiring them to register as foreign agents.

LARRY. Isn't that the same?

ZHUDOV. As you yourself wrote, the agents of the secret forces who control us. And this afternoon he congratulates a delegation from a small town in the east, the hundredth municipality to declare itself a LGBT-free zone.

LARRY. And he's built a razor-wire-topped fence across the southern border.

ZHUDOV. And bans abortion and gives tax breaks to expectant mothers. You will be delighted that he implements your platform quite so comprehensively. Is that it?

LARRY. Why shouldn't that be it?

ZHUDOV. I would have thought the jailing of his recent electoral opponent should feature in a list of his most egregious political atrocities.

LARRY. I thought that was overthrown by the Supreme Court.

ZHUDOV. Forgive me, there's no reason you should know.

LARRY. Know what?

ZHUDOV. In order to prevent it sabotaging your good work, there will be some changes in the make-up of the Supreme Court.

(*Looks at his watch.*) Have been, in fact.

LARRY (*standing*). So why on earth should I stay here?

ZHUDOV. I'd check your bank account.

LARRY *checks his account on his phone.*

Mr Yeates. Four years ago you converted Petr Lutsevic from a fumbling amateur to an orator of Rooseveltian proportions. So, no, we are not asking you to secure the re-election – of which there is no doubt – of the president of a minor Eastern European country. Instead, we propose that you magnify his reputation, as the leader of an international movement of resistance to the global forces you identified so effectively in the election. Any recent payments?

LARRY. There are. You're asking me to be his global reputation manager?

ZHUDOV. Oh much more than that. But to start, a new foundation, holding conferences, placing ghost-written op-ed articles, promoting the ideas and ideology which you pioneered. We thought of calling it the Stal'ko Group.

ZHUDOV pats the other end of the bench. LARRY sits.

LARRY. And second?

ZHUDOV. Naturally, to spread this message wider. Via the new means which the Global Lords of Cyberspace have so kindly provided us. Messages which pop up on our screens for a second and then disappear. The Clintons are killers. Soros is Sauron. No indication of the source, the cost, or who paid for them.

LARRY. Or if they're true.

ZHUDOV. So you don't think there's a conspiracy by a liberal elite? Whose aims include the transformation of your party from one dedicated to the cause of labour to one obsessed with the more demented reaches of feminism and gay rights? With the objective, clearly, to destroy the Christian family, in all senses? Maybe, even, yours?

LARRY. There were concerns about the language.

Enter PETR.

ZHUDOV. But not sufficient to provoke your resignation. And, as was proved, the language of conspiracy fits with the truth of how things look from Zlin and Stal'ko. And perhaps from southern Austria and northern France. The forgotten parts of England. Even upstate Michigan. And on that scale, do you really want your work undone?

Pause.

PETR (*to* ZHUDOV). Has he agreed?

LARRY stands.

LARRY. Mr President.

ZHUDOV looks to LARRY. PETR nods to the rifle. ZHUDOV hands him the rifle. PETR aims it. Is he going to fire it? Is he going to fire it at LARRY? *But he hands* LARRY *the rifle.*

PETR. So far, we are victorious. But we remember Sunflower. And Bulldozer and Orange and Carnation. And all the other 'revolutions' which have overthrown legitimately elected national leaders. If we want to keep this thing. And maybe, yes, to be a dictator for a day.

ZHUDOV (*to* PETR). And who brought about your victory? And where else might he work his magic?

(*To* LARRY.) And which other lands make great again?

PETR. Indeed. Enjoy.

He goes out. LARRY *stands with the rifle, looking at* ZHUDOV.

LARRY. And where next? Will you be deemed to be invaluable?

ZHUDOV. Transnistra? Georgia, eventually. Tomorrow, I expect Crimea.

Pause.

It was your platform. It was you who sold it to the populace. You believe in it. And, now, you have the chance to bring it home.

Scene Twelve

2016. August, upstate Michigan. A restaurant; the joint is jumping. LARRY *has entered.* RACHEL *– a little uncomfortable in her surroundings – is listening on speaker to an answerphone message. We hear and see* CARO's *message:*

CARO. Brexit referendum. Fifty-two per cent yes, forty-eight no. What started out in Zlin and Stal'ko ends up in Bolton, Bolsover and Burnley. The New Real. And do you forgive me? Do I forgive you?

LARRY *has entered.*

LARRY. Forgive you for what?

RACHEL *ends* CARO's *call and puts her phone on the table.*

RACHEL. 'Smoky Pete's Eat Place.'

LARRY. I won and I deserved it.

RACHEL. Well, you won.

LARRY. Check out the steaks. I've ordered you a 'G and T'.

RACHEL. Phil and I have taken to old fashioneds.

LARRY. 'Phil.' And you're working for Hillary.

RACHEL. And you're working for the self-styled illiberal president of a country rapidly careering to the authoritarian right.

LARRY. Who was elected and then re-elected. Whose policies are overwhelmingly endorsed in frequent referenda. Who's released his previous opponent from jail.

RACHEL. Now did I not read that in an op-ed in the *New York Times*?

LARRY. The *Post*. Conceivably.

RACHEL. Allegedly by a member of 'The Zlin Group'.

LARRY. Stal'ko. But I may not be working there for long.

RACHEL. Why not?

LARRY. I've been asked to work for someone else. Whose people read the *Post* piece, naturally.

Pause. RACHEL *knows.*

RACHEL. 'Someone else.'

LARRY. I worked for Obama. Now I'm working for a campaign which is hoovering up Obama voters because on so many economic issues they're on the same side.

RACHEL. He promises the biggest infrastructure programme since the New Deal. All he'd actually do is build his fucking wall. Gin but no Coke.

A male WAITER *appears with the drinks and dirty fries.*

WAITER. One 'gin and tonic'. One Cuba Libre. And some dirty fries.

RACHEL. Thanks.

WAITER. Now might I take your food / order?

RACHEL. Give us five.

WAITER. No problem.

He's headed out, when:

LARRY. Excuse me.

WAITER. Sir?

LARRY. Are you from a labour union family?

WAITER. I sure am.

LARRY. And your vote in 2012?

WAITER. I voted for President Obama.

LARRY. Why?

WAITER. He stood up for the auto industry.

LARRY. Any reservations?

WAITER. Well, I guess I could do without homosexuals in the military.

LARRY. And what did your father do when they closed the Buick plant?

WAITER. He filled vending machines. For a year or two.

LARRY. And who'll you be voting for this time?

Slight pause.

WAITER. The Idaho fillet is to die for.

The WAITER *goes out.*

RACHEL. And Trump's talking about Hillary having secret meetings with international bankers to enrich global financial powers.

LARRY. You don't think Hillary has secret meetings?

RACHEL. Echoing your disgraceful Schaefer line.

LARRY. But, in fact –

RACHEL. Which is why I'm here to stop you, Larry.

Pause.

LARRY. Oh. And how d'you reckon you'll do that?

RACHEL. When did you tell the US government you were working for a foreign power in the United States?

LARRY. When did you tell them you were working for Bezborodko?

RACHEL. I didn't need to, because I wasn't working for her in the United States. Which without informing the US goverment of that fact is a criminal offence, subject to a prison term of not more than five years, a fine of two hundred and fifty thousand dollars, or both.

LARRY. How can you prove I was?

She picks up her phone, switches off the recorder, and puts it in her bag. She stands.

RACHEL. Because you just told me. Not the *Times*, the *Post*. Not Zlin, Stal'ko. Which I now have taped. Illicitly.

She picks up her phone before LARRY *can get to it.*

LARRY. I just don't think you'd do that.

RACHEL. Really?

LARRY. Betcha. Because when it comes down to it, you're just too nice and smart and fun to skewer anyone like this would skewer me.

RACHEL. My mother. 'My fucking mother.' On the Freedom Rides. Part of a coalition. Not just black and white. My folks and your folks. Berkeley and Flint. Which brought about the New Deal and skewered Hitler. And eventually getting the US out of Vietnam, and even two guys kissing on a cake. Everything that's good and kind and – yes, sure – ethical about the last one hundred years. So you redrew the map, with Flint on one side, Berkeley on the other. Red against Green. Equality against equal rights. I wouldn't do this? Try me.

LARRY. I didn't write the Schaefer line.

RACHEL. And you expect me to believe that?

LARRY. And of course all this is me.

RACHEL. All this what?

LARRY. But in fact it was you redrew the map of politics with the nice rich dudes on one side and the nasty poor people on the other. Both of us. And you end up working for a candidate who stood on a platform of 'let markets rip'. Whatever that means for the rust belt, here or there.

RACHEL. What d'you mean?

LARRY. I mean in the schism between Berkeley and Flint, who filed for divorce? Who abandoned all those pointless people in their smokestacks with their disreputable views? Just so you could feel good about yourself. And wasn't that the biggest dirty trick of all?

RACHEL looks at LARRY. She dials a number.

RACHEL. Yes, of course, you're right. And if it's any comfort I don't feel good about myself at all.

RACHEL's call is answered.

(*Phone.*) Department of Justice? I'm calling to report a federal offence, under the Foreign Agents Registration Act of 1938. Correct. Sure, put me through.

LARRY. Really?

RACHEL. Everything I know.

Scene Thirteen

2018. The Garden of War Heroes. OLEG *meets* NATALIA.

OLEG (*Slavic language*). Doidokhte! [You came.]

NATALIA (*Slavic language*). Ti kaza graditnata na Voennite Geroi! [You said, the Garden of War Heroes.]

OLEG. You can say in English.

NATALIA. You said, 'When I return, we meet in the Garden of War Heroes.'

OLEG. For a while, a haunt of prostitutes and drug dealers. And the statues, covered in graffiti.

NATALIA. And now the graffiti is on mosques. And synagogues. And who was responsible for that.

OLEG. It wasn't me or Larry Yeates. It was our candidate.

NATALIA. But most effective nonetheless.

OLEG. Which is why I do not work for President Lutsevic.

NATALIA. Your grandfather dying to stop fascism.

OLEG. And I said we should come back here and make things work.

NATALIA. And now I live in London with my mother.

Slight pause.

OLEG. Do you remember what people told us? How smart young Americans would come and show us how to do democracy?

NATALIA. But instead of turning our country into his, we turn his country into ours. To 'make it great again'.

OLEG. And you wanted to choose any person you can be.

NATALIA. And I end up daughter of a former president.

They look at each other. A mordant little laugh between them.

OLEG. So what do we do now? To turn this thing around?

NATALIA. It's simple. Like my trumpet. You just blow.

Scene Fourteen

2022 or 2023 or 2024. Sounds of warfare in the near distance: shelling, bombs and planes. ZHUDOV, *in army fatigues, crawls onto the stage. He is seriously injured. Then he stands. He's not injured after all.*

ZHUDOV. So imagine all of this we have imagined.

That our politics is a hologram and yours a shadow play. And vice versa, naturally.

So that when protesters flood the streets and squares of our eastern capitals, we say that they are in the pay of Western powers.

And that secret forces plot to empty sovereign countries of their populations and replace them with another at their sole command.

And that, when we invade a country which does not exist but is controlled by Nazis and drug addicts, the atrocities that are committed there are fake.

And the invasion is not an invasion and the war is not a war.

That the people on the streets of Bishkek and Kyiv, Budapest and Tbilisi, are paid agitators, actors, hooligans and a mirage.

But that for all its manifest absurdity, all of the above is actually true and actually real.

ZHUDOV *realises something. He touches his stomach and looks at his hand. It's covered in blood.*

I need… I need you to believe this now.

Blackout.

End of play.

The Real of *The New Real*

1989 November 9	The fall of the Berlin Wall signals the end of communist regimes in East Germany, Hungary, Poland, Czechoslovakia, Bulgaria and Romania.
1991 August 19	In the Soviet Union, a coup by hardliners against the reforming government of Mikhail Gorbachev fails.
1991 December 25	Following the secession of Belarus, Ukraine, Kazakhstan and other former Soviet republics, the USSR ceases to exist. Boris Yelstin is president of an independent Russia.
1992 November	Bill Clinton defeats sitting President George H. W. Bush.
1993 October 4	Boris Yelstin dissolves, and then orders the army to shell the Russian parliament, claiming this is necessary to bring about market reforms. Over 100 die.
1996 July 7	Aided by Western strategists, Yeltsin wins the presidential election in a close race against the Communist Party.
1999 March 12	Hungary, Poland and Czechoslovakia join NATO.
1999 August	Vladimir Putin becomes prime minister of Russia, and then acting president, when Yeltsin steps down at the end of the year.
2000 February	In Austria, the post-fascist Freedom Party wins 27% of the vote and enters government for the first time.

2000 September 26	The US government sues Harvard University, claiming that Harvard staff enriched themselves while aiding free market reforms in Russia.
2000 October	In Serbia, the Bulldozer Revolution overthrows President Milosevic, following a fraudulent presidential election.
2000 November	George W. Bush beats Al Gore for president in the electoral college but not the popular vote.
2003 November 3	Georgia's Rose Revolution overthrows President Edward Shevardnadze, following accusations of election fraud.
2004 May	Ukraine's Ruslana wins the Eurovision Song Contest.
2004 November	In Ukraine, protests against the pro-Russian Viktor Yanukovych's rigging of the presidential election lead to the Orange Revolution and a new election.
2005 February	The Cedar Revolution in Lebanon is followed by the Tulip Revolution in Kyrgystan.
2008 September 15	The collapse of Lehman Brothers leads to a global economic crash, which hits Eastern European economies particularly badly.
2008 November	Barack Obama defeats John McCain in the US presidential race.
2010 January	In the Ukraine presidential election, Viktor Yanukovych is advised by US strategist Paul Manafort and Yulia Tymoshenko by David Axelrod. Yanukovych wins with 37% of the vote.

CHRONOLOGY 123

2010 April	Hungary's Viktor Orban wins a massive electoral victory on a national-populist progamme. He redraws electoral districts and limits the independence of the judiciary.
2011 December 4	Flawed elections in Russia lead to 80,000 people demonstrating in Moscow's Bolotnaya Square.
2012 August	Members of the Russian Pussy Riot protest group are jailed for two years for insulting religious sensitivities by protesting in church.
2013 November	In Ukraine, Yanukovych pulls out of the EU Association Agreement, leading to mass protests in Kyiv's Maidan Square.
2014 February	At the height of Maidan protests, Russia invades Crimea. Two days later, many protesters and some police are killed in Maidan Square. President Yanukovych resigns and flees.
2014 April 7	Pro-Russian People's Republics are proclaimed in Donetsk and Luhansk in eastern Ukraine.
2015 February 7	Putin critic Boris Nemtsov is assassinated in Moscow.
2015 October	Poland's centrist Civic Platform loses to the right-wing Law and Justice Party, which politicises civil service and judiciary, and imposes an almost total ban on abortion.
2016 June 23	The UK votes to leave the European Union in the Brexit referendum.
2016 August 19	Paul Manafort resigns as campaign manager of the Donald Trump presidential campaign, and is subsequently jailed.

2016 November	Donald Trump defeats Hillary Clinton in the US presidential election.
2019 December 12	In the UK general election, Boris Johnson's Conservatives make heavy gains in previously Labour 'red wall' seats and wins an 80-seat majority.
2021 January 6	Following Joe Biden's victory, President Trump incites his supporters to invade the Capitol to overturn the result.
2022 February 24	Russia invades Ukraine in a special military operation.
2022 April 24	In France, National Rally's Marine le Pen wins 41% of the vote in the run-off against President Macron.
2024 June 9	In the EU elections, the far right comes first in Italy, Austria and France, and defeats all the governing parties in Germany.

www.nickhernbooks.co.uk

facebook.com/nickhernbooks

twitter.com/nickhernbooks